REMEMBER TO SMILE

REMEMBER TO SMILE:
Looking for Kate

Elizabeth Osborne

HAYLOFT PUBLISHING LTD
CUMBRIA

Published by Hayloft Publishing Ltd., 2018

A CIP catalogue record for this book is available from the British Library

ISBN 978-1-910237-38-0

Designed, printed and bound in the EU

Hayloft policy is to use papers that are natural, renewable and recyclable products and
made from wood grown in sustainable forests. The logging and manufacturing
processes are expected to conform to the
environmental regulations of the country of origin.

This book is printed with the offset of carbon
emissions by additional carbon offset projects.
Supported offset project: Forest Protection, Pará, Brazil

Hayloft Publishing Ltd,
a company registered in England number 4802586
2 Staveley Mill Yard, Staveley, Kendal, LA8 9LR (registered office)
L'Ancien Presbytère, 21460 Corsaint, France (editorial office)

Email: books@hayloft.eu
Tel: 07971 352473
www.hayloft.eu

Frontispiece image: Kate, aged 25

To Patrick, Christian, Kate, Ruth, Poppy, Charlie, Arthur and Honor, who have been, and remain my raison d'etre; and to Jen and Robert, my sister and her husband

Christian, Kate and Ruth, Easter 1989.

CONTENTS

Elizabeth and Kate

FOREWORD

Sometimes you come across a book you cannot put down. *Remember to Smile: Looking for Kate* is one such book. It's a story which is at once compelling, tragic, true and celebratory. It is also beautifully written. This book is particularly special for me because I know Kate's family and I feel hugely privileged to have been invited to write the foreword.

Who else but a mother could present such a vivid portrait of this remarkable young woman, taken from her family far too soon and in such distressing circumstances. And in telling her daughter's story, she also tells her own. As Elizabeth writes with such insight and affection, from her earliest days, Kate was brilliantly different. She was an inquisitive child – adventurous, independent and talented, but always with a deep vein of compassion and love. Kate at all times tried to help those who might be down on their luck. She seemed to have an affinity for the vulnerable in any society, the outsiders, the lonely and the lost. As she grew to adulthood, her rebellious, big-hearted spirit tried it all, exploring the world and testing the boundaries, a world of increasing risk and danger, a danger that finally grew beyond her control.

I find this book completely compelling. It could so easily have just been the story of an impulsive, wilful child who flew too close to the flame. But it isn't. There is as much to admire in Kate as there is to criticise. She lived dangerously but selflessly and always with the desire both to see the best in others and to try to help them. It is a story of which every parent will say, 'That could have been the story of our child.' The nightmare scenario of drugs and violence to which so many can be attracted and be so terribly hurt. *There but for the Grace of God, go I*. It could also be a story of utter tragedy. But it isn't. Partly because throughout her life, Kate was so consistently kind, so honest, so compassionate, so caring. Her effect on the family was and remains remarkable. Always, they share their pain, always they are there for each other in a spirit not just of despair but of love, even pride.

Kate was a serious traveller, visiting places at the far reaches of the world that ordinary tourists will never see. She was a natural travel writer, and kept the family enthralled with her adventures. Elizabeth has included many of Kate's letters here, so we get to hear her 'speak' for herself. These letters are masterpieces in their own right; vibrant vignettes of how she feels, what she sees, and what she believes. One is left with a sense of a beautiful, questing spirit, always seeking but never quite finding her place in the world, quick to laugh, and always there for others. In a particularly poignant episode, we see her volunteering her language skills to help families identify the victims of the Bali bombings in 2002.

Kate was an idealist, and while the world needs such people the world invariably uses them very harshly. Her final cause was always going to be a lost one, but whether or not we, as readers, parents, or friends of the family might not agree, or even understand, Kate believed in it, and it destroyed her.

Seven hundred people came to her memorial service at St. Cuthbert's Church in Carlisle. Family and friends, of course, but many professionals, too, who had been involved in Kate's story and who had been deeply moved by her plight and that of her family, who never gave up searching for answers. All of them came not just to say farewell but to celebrate and to say thank you to a woman whose courage, compassion, energy and kindness had moved them deeply.

This book tells that story and I cannot commend it too highly.

Bishop John Richardson, Bewcastle
December 2017

CELEBRATION

Saturday 17 April 2004 and my husband Patrick was standing at the lectern, giving the address we had pored over long and hard.

'Trust Kate to bring out the sun. She would have revelled in this today, surrounded by family and friends, good music, and afterwards a party at The Tithe Barn. That's if she made it on time. Punctuality was not her strongest point!'

We were gathered to celebrate the life of the adventurous feisty daughter who was no longer with us. In part this service was to mark acceptance of the fact that she was not coming back, but it was also in response to the hundreds of letters we had received since her disappearance in Bali in April 2003, exactly twelve months before. So many cards, notes, postcards and heartfelt letters. She touched so many lives.

Approaching the church in Carlisle I felt tense and apprehensive. We hired a minibus so the extended family could all travel together from home but we were pretty subdued. There was blue sky but it was a raw, freezing day. I was surrounded by family. There was my husband Patrick, Christian and Ruth my daughters, my sister Jen, all of whom had been so strong and supportive during the past year, but I could not rise above the feeling that I just did not want to be here. This was an occasion I should not have to go through.

We chose St Cuthbert's Church in Carlisle because of its size and central location, but I was stunned nevertheless by the huge queue of people waiting to enter. When we were planning this I had no idea how many to expect. I would later hear that about seven hundred people attended the service.

There were so many faces, it was hard to take them all in. Family, school friends, work mates, long-time neighbours, old family friends from Cumbria and elsewhere, and Kate's friends from her travels.

There were some people we had never met before but whose lives intertwined with hers. They had come from London, all over Europe, Canada, America and beyond. I wanted to stop and say hello to everyone, to thank them for being there. My son-in-law Francis had to come out of the church and escort me inside because the service was just about to start.

Having been outside the church for so long, I had missed all the classical music we had spent hours deliberating on, trying to find pieces which Kate liked that struck the right balance so that people felt uplifted as they came in. We spent even longer choosing the hymns – 'Sing out my Soul', 'Love Divine', 'Lord of all Hopefulness', 'Jerusalem'.

We wanted something familiar, something people would feel confident enough to join in with. Those who knew Kate only as a party girl, a world traveller, were surprised by some of the music that was played, but she also had a very traditional side.

I had bought a new suit for the occasion, in a pink and grey hounds-tooth check. I had it slightly altered, the neckline seemed too low-cut, given the occasion, and so I asked them in the shop to put a hook and eye on it. I dreaded the shop assistant enquiring what it was for, as they do. If I'd had to answer that, I might have burst into tears. It was a good two-piece, smart but not too formal. I felt strong in it. It was important to find something that made me feel at my best.

Canon Richard Pratt, the vicar, reminded us that St Cuthbert's is more than just a building; it is a place where, for centuries, the people of Carlisle have brought their joys and their sorrows. A place to be silent and remember.

I sat quietly doing just that. It was not difficult to summon up images of Kate; she was a force of nature – vibrant, full of laughter and mischief, impossible to contain even if you had wanted to. On the back of the Order of Service was a collage of images of her many different roles – daughter, sister, doting aunt, horsewoman, back-packer, intrepid traveller.

I glanced around the church which was packed, there were even people standing in the gallery. We were literally surrounded by family and friends, hundreds of them, willing us to come through and there for Kate.

I was always the one to discipline our three girls. I laughed and cried, with and for them, fastidious in their upbringing. Patrick was often unaware of the scraps, the escapades, the embarrassed apologies, the brushes with the law. But we did have fun. Patrick was the breadwinner with a very stressful job, so I tried to keep the girls' trials and tribulations under wraps, as far as possible. This will resonate with many women whose husbands are wedded to their job. It is not because they are not wholly committed to their family. They simply have a different take on it, as they do other aspects of life, like the way they grieve, and Patrick does have his own way of dealing with Kate's death, as I do. One of many things we have in common is an unconditional love of all our daughters.

One thing I left with Patrick was to speak for both of us in our tribute to Kate at St Cuthbert's. An awesome, gut wrenching and heart breaking task. I was grateful to him for being so courageous in his determination to do it. Together we composed what he would say.

PART ONE

1

EARLY LIFE

Our second daughter Kate was born on the morning of 13 May 1968. I was 24 years old and it was an easy birth, delivered by my own GP in the nearby Cottage Hospital in Brampton, North Cumbria. Our older daughter, Christian, was then two.

By the age of three, unlike Christian who had been the most easy going child, Kate had become extremely clingy, dreaded being left anywhere, so I had to give up on the idea of play school where she simply screamed. She hated me leaving her.

Looking back it seems surprising that this same child subsequently adventured, explored, learned foreign languages, often on her own, all over the world.

Once back in the safety of her home, Kate could play for hours by herself. Lorries, tractors, horse boxes, trucks and Lego construction were her passion. Fiercely protective of her small fleet of vehicles, on one occasion when a little boy came to play and broke her Land Rover, she was ready to kill him. She was showing signs of developing a formidable temper. Was this the notorious three year old tantrums or a portent for the future?

When Kate was about three, Dorothy, my mother-in-law, fell badly on the stairs in her home. She was living in Raughton Head, a hamlet near Carlisle, 40 minutes' drive from us. As a result of her fall she ended up in a spinal unit in Sheffield with a broken neck. This facility, where she remained for a year's treatment and rehabilitation, was more than two and a half hours from our home near Brampton, a five hour round trip on Sundays.

The accident compounded the most difficult aspects of Dorothy's nature. She was the most negative person I had ever met; dealing with this situation was going to be very, very challenging.

She was full of bitterness about everything; from her childhood when she felt she had been hard done by and bore grudges about the most trivial things; envy of other people who socialised with ease, and now of course people who could walk and lead so called 'normal' lives. Many friends and acquaintances made a big effort with her but she was so rude to them that they eventually decided not to go back for more.

A few years later when Dorothy had to go into a nursing home we had to learn to live with the constant threat of her being turned out because she was so difficult.

Patrick was her only child and his father, Frank, had been killed during war service, an event she could never bring herself to speak about. She married again, unhappily, but had a longed for daughter, Tana. Dorothy's life was one long, continuing disappointment; her only comfort was the company of her daughter and son, my husband, whom she felt she owned. She was jealous of the demands made by the other females in his life and resented them enormously. Hugely sensitive to her own needs, she was almost entirely insensitive to the needs of others. As a result she expected an all-day visit, at least once over the weekend during the year of her long hospitalisation.

I made a short-lived attempt to make the visits a family affair. We sat round the hospital bed and it was very strained. Kate was particularly curious. When she saw the plastic container at the end of the catheter she asked, 'Is that granny's orange juice?' All her life she was nothing if not direct.

Having abandoned the family visits we then left Christian and Kate with a few very good friends. This happened most weekends for a year and Kate hated it. It did nothing to heal her insecurity. Christian was wonderful as a substitute mother but it was very distressing. Because of the situation with my mother-in-law, we asked the nuns at the excellent convent primary school where Christian was thriving if they would take Kate in earlier than usual, to which they agreed.

At the outset she was very excited to be going to the big school with her sister, but soon a pattern developed which involved sore tummy and headaches in the morning, plus sleepless nights. She'd

Kate's Christening.

had night terrors when she was very young and would be taken screaming into our bed in the small hours. Little was known about this phenomenon then, and not much more now. Although this had improved with time, the broken night's sleep still obstinately remained. When I took her to our doctor and explained how exhausting our lives had become he suggested putting her on Phenobarbitone, a barbiturate, which I declined. I thought there must be some way of helping her other than a sedative. We did not give her any medicine and eventually she outgrew the problem.

After a term or so I asked the Sisters with some trepidation how Kate behaved in school and they responded that she was quiet in class, sometimes seemed to be in a world of her own. They wondered whether she could be a little deaf? But she was popular and had made friends. The other children liked her and she was no trouble. Sometime later I reflected that these problems were caused by a fundamental sense of insecurity, and I think that sending her to school too soon was not helpful.

Outside school she was a different child, an absolute tomboy. She had explosive energy; all was wonderful one moment and the next you didn't know what had hit you. Food became a vital part of her routine and I eventually took sandwiches for her to eat straight out of school. I realized she was one of those children who needed to eat regularly and at this time her sugar levels must have been all over the place.

Christian and Kate ready for school

Physically, Kate was tiny, doll-like; a girl who loved cuddles, was passionate about bedtime stories, but would not read a book. Throughout her formal education she was never an enthusiastic reader. She was exceptionally creative from an early age, demonstrating a singular artistic talent and a vivid imagination. I think she was one of those people whose education seriously began after she left school, when she read avidly, including some quite esoteric even cerebral material.

When Christian was seven a great family friend asked her to be her bridesmaid, and in order that Kate, aged five, should not feel excluded, Bridget thoughtfully organized a posy for her to hold at the wedding.

Kate, always wanting to be wherever her sister was, followed her around all day, caught up in the excitement until the photographer had to take the bridesmaids away for the photo shoot. To his embarrassment Kate threw a complete wobbly, refusing to be parted from Christian. I was unaware of what was happening, taking the opportunity to catch up with old friends. Then I heard a high-pitched wail, 'You can't do that. I'm a bridesmaid too!'

To his credit the photographer took the time to coax Kate away to have her photograph taken on her own with her posy, and we have a picture of her, tearful and forlorn, to remind us of the drama. I was so grateful to him for managing to divert attention and save the day. Unlike my temper, which was lost when not getting my own way, Kate's was expressed when she perceived injustice.

In 1976 something was to happen to change our family life dramatically. I became pregnant, rather unexpectedly, and Ruth was born on 8 December. Christian was almost eleven and Kate nine. The older girls were thrilled with the new addition to the family.

Ponies figured hugely in both Christian and Kate's lives, and in the holidays they frequently packed lunch in a saddlebag and rode over the fells all day, oblivious of time. We picnicked, swam, walked, talked endlessly and enjoyed time in Hampshire with my sister and brother-in-law, Jen and Robert, and their children, Peter and Elizabeth. We would drive to Eurocamp in the Pyrenees together, cars packed to the gunwales and there were wonderful holidays cruising the waterways on canal boats and memorable visits to a small chateau in the Dordogne.

We frequently used my grandmother's house in the Lake District as a bolthole. Gaga, as my grandmother was affectionately known, was a warm wonderful hostess and adored the children. The Gale was a thirteen-bedroomed country house where my brother Anthony, Jen and I had largely grown up when my parents went off to live wherever the RAF posted them. My grandmother had downsized in recent years from the big house to a much smaller one in the village and when we visited we were packed in together like sardines.

Although she no longer had the money and lifestyle she had known, the people who had worked as staff in the old days continued to look after her as they always had. For me, just being in the Lake District brought back so many happy memories – it was where my siblings and I had grown up with the freedom one could enjoy in those days and which I wanted with a passion for my own children. There is no doubt, though, we were fairly wild. The fundamental requirements in my day were good manners and a social awareness and that is something I tried to instil in my girls too, however, such freedom came at a price.

Around this age we started to notice that Kate had little or no sense of time. We bought her a watch to see if that would make a difference, but she forgot to wear it. Punctuality was to remain a problem throughout Kate's life, which could be infuriating and caused havoc on occasions.

She was about ten when a favourite great aunt died and she was determined to come to the funeral with the rest of us. I told her well in advance and reiterated at intervals the time we must leave the house. She was not ready. So we left her, in a ferocious temper, in the hands of a woman who helped out and knew the children well.

Insecurity continued to manifest itself now and again – she had an outward appearance of confidence, but that belied the truth. When she was ten I was called out on two separate occasions to pick her up from what should have been sleepovers with friends. In each case the mothers wisely thought it preferable to pre-empt a potentially sleepless night by alerting me about 10 p.m. rather than the early hours of the morning should things become more trying.

Aged twelve, academically quite bright, tall and athletic, very good at sport, spirited, with a lot of charm but always to the point, she was popular with pupils and staff. There were many mischievous pranks,

Kate aged five with her wedding posy.

but nothing outrageous. She always had a great sense of fun.

She had a good friend, Emily, with whom she was at school locally for two years. She brought her home from time to time. They were very alike, particularly in time keeping which meant double trouble. My mother, very game but rather frail and quite elderly, was looking after the household in our absence and agreed that the girls could take a picnic lunch and walk over the fell as long as they were back for tea. At 8 p.m. they arrived home to a frantic grandmother, having absolutely no idea, so lost in talk were they, of the worry they had caused. Emily tragically died at seventeen when she fell from a cliff during a holiday job which left a very deep impression on Kate. I think the first death a young person has to deal with is profoundly traumatic in any circumstance, provoking intense emotions that are not necessarily understood.

Kate, now a regular teenager, if indeed there is any such thing, was

Kate and Christian with baby Ruth.

frustrated in Cumbria, and she longed to join Christian in Edinburgh. When she was fourteen and close to taking her GCSEs at the local school, Kate broke up for the Christmas holidays and announced that she was not going back to 'that crap school' and implored us to let her join her sister at Fettes College in Edinburgh. Unfortunately Fettes did not have space, so I contacted St George's.

The headmistress was reluctant, even more so when I told her the school she had been attending, because apparently their standards were 'not on a par with theirs'. I subsequently read in St George's prospectus that 'we do not tolerate failure'. I must have been very persuasive because the headmistress said Kate could sit the entrance exam on the first day of the following term. We would have the results at the end of the day but she was not expected to pass.

She surprised us by achieving good results in all subjects, much to the headmistress's astonishment, and that same afternoon I found myself buying the uniform for Kate to start at St George's the following day. I felt it vindicated the local school as it had a great headmaster who had seen the girls' potential and done extremely well by both of them.

St George's, like Fettes, did not have a bed available but she was invited to live with her friend Jessica and her sister in Ann Street, a lovely part of Edinburgh. It was to be board and lodging, with me visiting regularly to keep an eye on things. I was uneasy about the arrangement as Kate was still so young. But she already showed a fiercely independent streak and in the end I allowed myself to be swayed by her persuasive arguments.

She came home frequently on the train bringing friends, and on one occasion a kitten that got loose in the carriage. She seemed to be coping; it was not ideal but probably suited her temperament rather more than living in a boarding house at school. She quickly made friends: Jessica, with whom she lived, and her younger sister Becky; Francesca or Cheesie who was to figure largely, on and off, for the rest of Kate's life – and beyond; Iona, Mairi, Jeanine, Floss and Kirsten who had been on the periphery but came back into the picture when Kate was in her twenties in London.

Iona had apparently befriended Kate on her first day at the school thinking she was shy and retiring. Over the next few weeks, she had revised her first opinion and pronounced that Kate was, without doubt, 'the cheekiest girl in the whole school – streets ahead of the rest of them'. For me it was great to hear that Kate was having fun and enjoying herself, but I made a note to find out if the teachers shared this view at the next parents' evening.

Another friend who came on to the scene around this time was Mairi. She had arrived at St George's in the same year, but unlike Kate, not mid-way through the term. She said Kate's arrival had caused a cloud of speculation. Why had she moved school? Where had she come from? Had she been chucked out? – which Kate did little to dispel. Mairi described the place as a 'stifling Miss Jean Brodie type school not best suited to those with a bit of fire in their blood' (among whom she included herself and Kate). She said that Kate was a breath of fresh air – she didn't appear to give a fig about authority and consequently drove the uptight, bunned and tweed-suited women of a certain age totally mad. Hilarious and disruptive, Kate in Mairi's view, was a free spirit who seemed to be oblivious of the effect she had on people.

Francesca – Cheesie as she was known – was Kate's absolute best friend. They were so close they were almost like sisters. But just like sisters they had explosive arguments that spilled over into the rest of the group, then fizzled out as if nothing had happened.

Kate had her own unique way of customizing the rather staid St George's uniform. She wore over-the-knee socks, two rust-red cardigans (rather than the usual one), the lower one buttoned up like a waistcoat under the other, and the skirt hitched up and stapled to take it considerably shorter than the regulation length. She had an old silver fork made into a kind of choker around her neck and always wore brightly coloured friendship bands around her wrists.

The wildness and mischief at school were something I could relate to; I too had been a rebel and had endless letters written home about my behaviour. I remember once swinging churns round and over my head in an attempt to prove that the milk would not come out. I persuaded other tables to do the same. There was not a happy outcome but we had a lot of laughs. On another occasion I led the dining room out on strike over the disgusting food. When Kate was fourteen we decided to move house. Raysdale had been the most wonderful home when the girls were little, situated as it was in the middle of the village of Castle Carrock, with a large garden, but as Christian, Kate and Ruth grew older we found we needed more space.

When Black Dub came on the market, Patrick saw its potential immediately despite the rusting farm machinery and old fertilizer bags that greeted one on arrival. It was a few miles outside Brampton, in the middle of nowhere, up for quick sale because the owner had over-extended himself financially. Dub is a Scottish word for marshland, which holds peat and it certainly fitted that definition. Although it was very run-down, the house itself was in reasonable shape, more importantly it came with substantial outbuildings and twelve acres of land. It would be hard work, but it had much potential – grazing land, stables, plenty of bedrooms, privacy. We talked through the drawbacks – years of hard work to civilize the house and garden, the fact that it was relatively cut off and the girls were becoming more interested in social life. In the end we convinced ourselves it was meant to be.

In 1981 we bought Black Dub. Built of local sandstone, it is a Victorian farmhouse and steading with a courtyard. Its appearance was rather austere, but is now tempered by wonderful views and an attractive garden with shrubs and trees.

Patrick realized a dream when an engineering friend dug out the two acre dub and developed a wonderful small lake with three islands. The atmosphere is a little reminiscent of *Swallows and Amazons*.

Kate had a lot of freedom in Edinburgh – way too much, in retrospect. She eked out the allowance we gave her, ostensibly to go to the pictures, but as I later found out, used it to go clubbing, often with her friend Mairi. Since neither of them had family nearby giving them the third degree, they were able to lie about where they were going and get away with it. As they got older and continued to go clubbing in the city, Kate was always the one pushing to go to bigger and better parties. She loved dancing with a passion. It was the start of her 'adventuring' and she would apparently happily get into cars with strangers if she thought there was fun to be had, even if her friends had decided to cry off. At the time I believed she was simply indulging her obsession with art-house cinema.

During school holidays we gave lots of parties. Entertaining had always played a large part in our upbringing, so I was determined my girls would have a good and varied social life. It was obvious when we acquired Black Dub that we would have to bring the fun to us, and so we did. We had numerous parties in the large barn at Christmas or New Year, birthdays and Bank Holidays, we didn't really need much excuse. In fact Kate became extremely adept at decking out the barn on the cheap, often from scraps we had lying around, or greenery she foraged from the hedgerows, sometimes painting murals on the walls.

In Cumbria, probably typical of many rural counties, these parties were often family affairs where you might find three generations at the same gathering. Ever forthright, at one such party given for the great and the good locally, Kate's eyes lit on a singularly opulent signet ring worn by rather an arrogant gentleman. To my horror she enquired whether he had bought it at House of Fraser, which rendered him temporarily speechless. Of course it had been in his family for centuries. I was never sure if the question was tongue-in-cheek or not.

On one occasion we took a party to the Westmorland Ball, held near Newby Bridge – a long way away – which necessitated three car-loads of teenagers being transported. Christian was one of the drivers, but had such a good time that she was unable to drive home. Kate was a learner driver and had not been drinking, and as we had no option we reluctantly agreed to give her the responsibility. She took it seriously and approached a friend of ours for advice as to how best she could avoid motorways, and traffic, explaining that she hadn't yet passed her test. He duly recommended the best route, which he was well qualified to do as he was working in the area; it wasn't until the following morning over a late breakfast that we enlightened her with the fact he was a police inspector!

There were to-ings and fro-ings with sleeping bags under the arm

*Kate, in 1984,
aged sixteen.*

and both girls having a lot of fun. If they were away overnight, I insisted on contact numbers and often rang the parents of the house where they were staying. Much of this fun rubbed off on us because they frequently brought friends home. While we were having all this fun we always tried to imbue the children – fast becoming young adults – with a sense of morals. I was prepared to be open-minded with the girls about most things, but there were rules.

On another occasion Kate embarked for Edinburgh to stay for 24 hours. Although she didn't have a phone number, she did have an address and Christian knew the boy she would be staying with which was helpful. Looking back, we relied quite often on Christian when it came to Kate's socializing in Edinburgh. If Christian knew the person in question it was fine. If she didn't, we felt we had no choice but to refuse. On this occasion the visit was given the all clear. We agreed Kate would ring me the following day with her train arrival time back in Carlisle.

The next day came and went and I found myself moving from mild annoyance to extreme worry, to out and out fury. I was so angry a further 24 hours later that, although I didn't really believe Kate was in trouble, I rang the Edinburgh police, who were extremely helpful. They called round at the address I had been given, found no-one at home, but left a note for Kate to contact them and ring me. She did this a few hours later and got a broadside. I was incandescent with rage, how dare she behave like this? She was very cross that we had called the police, oblivious to the turmoil she had caused. It hadn't occurred to her that we might be going out of our minds with worry, and there was no mystery or drama or even a good excuse. She had just got swept up in things; she was having too good a time.

As I write this, I am aware how much this seems like a foretaste of the future. Eighteen years later there was not to be a conclusion with anger, relief, and eventually forgiveness and hugs. I can't remember what precipitated it, but when she was sixteen Patrick turned to me after one or other of these ding-dongs and just said, 'What are we going to do about Kate?'

Patrick felt we needed to establish some new ground rules with our daughter. We had accepted by now that she had her own time clock, and that it wasn't the same as anyone else's. Something would catch her eye and she'd be gone – lost. We decided that we had to cease doing battle with her and everything had to be up for discussion.

A-levels loomed menacingly on the horizon. Despite my frequent visits to Edinburgh, the distractions of the city were proving too much, and while St George's reassured us that Kate had what it took exam-wise, I could see the way things were going. I kept repeating, 'You need to work, you're running out of time.' But it fell on deaf ears. Kate was not particularly confident academically, but neither was she a reviser. It wasn't because she was blasé about her chances; she was enjoying too many extracurricular activities.

On the day the results came out, Francesca was staying with us at Black Dub. When the postman arrived I was out with the dogs. Kate had failed her Highers and Francesca had passed. Kate's pride had been seriously hurt and she was very, very angry. This was Kate's first experience of failure and she remained angry for days but flatly refused to re-sit the examinations.

Patrick had often been approached about giving the girls holiday jobs at Cavaghan & Gray, the firm where he was a director. There was strong resistance on his part, although most of the board had organized work for their offspring at some time or other. Patrick didn't believe in nepotism, not that the moral aspect was his only consideration. He was very wary of Kate's legendary time keeping, and he did say that, if she let him down, he would never forgive her.

Eventually, though, Kate's desire to buy a new bike won him over and he was persuaded to allow her to apply to the appropriate office. The company, originally a bacon-curing factory, owned farms which produced pigs – the basic raw material. In recent years it had invested heavily in recipe dish production. These new products were trialled in a handful of stores, with sales being carefully monitored, and, if deemed successful, quickly supplied nationally.

Kate did not want people to know she was a director's daughter. She applied for employment in a nearby associated factory making skinless sausages to go with baked beans for a national canning company. To keep up the pretence, Patrick would drop her off for her shift at 6am well out of sight of the satellite factory where she was to work. Kate loved the endless ribaldry, almost certainly picking up even more undesirable vocabulary and generally having a ball. A whole host of jokes came home, most of which completely baffled me. She was never late, and nobody ever realized who she was. It was a good summer, but Kate did say she wouldn't want to do it for the rest of her life. On her final day she was thrown into a vat of iced sausages with the greatest good humour.

With her new bike, Kate and her best mate Francesca announced that they were going on a cycling holiday round Norfolk, that being the obvious choice because of the flat terrain. They went by train, panniers stuffed with kit. On arrival it was pouring with rain. They cycled for about two miles and, according to the postcards we later received, 'holed up in some naff B&B for the night'. They then proceeded to spend two nights at an awful caravan park. They did not stay long.

Rupert Younger, a friend from Scotland, later told me that they had turned up at his flat on Belgrave Road in Pimlico, completely out of the blue. Parking their muddy bikes in his entrance hall, the girls asked if they could crash there. What could he say, having heard their tall tales of cycling horrors and seen the war wounds on their legs? The flat had a small balcony, the weather was brilliant, they drank, smoked and talked into the night and sat in the sunshine in the day just 'recuperating'. He later wrote to me that it was a time of 'great friendship and great conversation... I will always have in my mind's eye an image of Kate smiling, with that mesmerizing twinkle in her eyes.'

Kate had no idea what she wanted to do next. Her friends were all going off to university or college. Some would walk straight into jobs; such things were still possible in the early 1980s. At her request we went to a reputable careers adviser in London where she was interviewed and sat a psychometric test designed to form a profile of her strengths and weaknesses and suggest possible careers accordingly. She was there for half a day.

We were sent a report; the three major strengths were her ability to relate to people, her practicality, and creativity. I can't remember what the downsides were, but I'm sure there were some. Accordingly the strengths could be channelled into psychology, mechanics, navigation in the RAF, marketing and lastly photography. It told us little—other than photography, which did become a passion later, nothing had huge appeal for her.

By late August a plan was starting to form. She was interested in art, and she had a strong enough portfolio to consider applying for a place on the foundation course at Carlisle Art College which had long been highly regarded. We were delighted at this positive turn and encouraged her to try.

She was given a place for six months – the duration of the course, the idea being to introduce students to many aspects of art, jewellery-making, sculpture in wood and metal, graphics, life drawing, photography, and more, in order to help them make a choice as to which area to pursue at degree level. She threw herself into the role of art student. She still lived in jeans, but these had become subtly more grungy. Keen to fit in, she insisted that Patrick drop her off a suitable distance from the gates of the college for fear of the Volvo and Barbour being seen.

Kate proved to be quite successful at graphics and good at drawing, and did enjoy the photography. However, at the end of the course she said there was no way she was going to spend another three years in an educational establishment pursuing a degree. She'd had enough of school. Her godfather, my brother-in-law, gave all his nephews, nieces, and godchildren a cheque on their eighteenth birthday for the return fare to travel. They were expected to pay their own way once abroad. This seemed like a good opportunity for Kate to get a different perspective on life and try to make a decision about her future. The plan was to travel to Canada with Francesca, touring around as much as they could. We felt Canada was as safe as anywhere for their first venture abroad, as both families had contacts there.

In order to raise the money to travel for a few months, Kate went to London where Christian was already working as personal assistant to the managing director of David Hicks, an interior design company. Christian managed to persuade them to give Kate a job on reception, answering the phone and running the occasional errand. My sister, Jen, allowed her to stay at their flat in Jubilee Place off the Kings Road to keep her costs to the minimum. It was quite a glamorous introduction to London life, though not a cheap part of town to be living in. Kate was delighted when she got her first wages.

We saw Kate and Francesca off to Canada with some apprehension on our part and eager anticipation on theirs. On arrival in Toronto Kate and Francesca were met by a cousin of mine, Charles Wakefield, in his stereotypically large Oldsmobile car. He and his family showed them around the city, were extremely hospitable, and probably rather shocked when the girls decided to buy a vibrant yellow, very old American banger for ninety dollars. It made a large hole in their hard-earned cash but made sense. They took a crash course in mechanics from the vendor. Francesca held the only driving licence, so she was to be the designated driver and Kate, who had failed her test twice, was to do running repairs. In fact they shared the driving.

They set off to drive from Toronto to Vancouver, and from Vancouver through the Rockies to Banff, exploring en route. They became adept at adjusting the piston timer. They stayed in hostels or camped and met a number of interesting fellow travellers, a very cosmopolitan crowd. They hired bikes and saw as much as they possibly could, and they partied, of course.

When they were introduced to a friend of a friend in a wheelchair, Kate asked in her inimitable way, 'So what happened to your legs?' to which he responded perfectly matter of factly. She took a photograph of a prairie rat sitting at the base of his wooden legs – the joke being that he would gnaw through them. Kate could be very direct, and artless, but with her charm she got away with it.

After numerous attempts, she managed to get a late-night job cleaning a shopping mall as well as the loos in a nightclub. It involved some travelling from the hostel so she decided, foolishly, to drive the car. One night, with the streets quiet, she finished work and driving home found she was being followed by the Mounties. Did she realize Banff was the training college for the Royal Canadian Mounted Police?

She pulled into a side street, switching off her lights – she must have been watching too many films – and waited until she felt safe enough to venture forth, only to find they had waited for her. She was stopped and asked for identification, whereupon in a panic she gave Francesca's name, but had no idea of her birth date. Unable to produce the necessary documentation, she was escorted back to the hostel where it all fell apart. However, it turned out the Mounties had suspected her of being an illegal immigrant, with her long, dark, tightly curled hair, and her tanned, slightly olive, skin. When she produced her own papers they thankfully told her not to work again without a permit, and left.

18 August 1987

Dear Mummy, Daddy, Christian and Ruth

Having a wonderful time, jobs are both going well, with good people, with good sense of humour. Got paid yesterday so went out for a meal today with a friend.

Weather has been very British recently with thunder, lightening, sun tan hasn't even started yet but hopefully when we get back east it will! Wish you hadn't told me it would be hot out here – I've spent the last few weeks scrounging clothes from 'fellow hostellers'.

Kate had run up an assortment of garments before leaving home, all cotton.

Both of us are becoming fairly cosmic with 'earth meetings' (man) and campfires and most of the people we meet seem to have a guitar stuck away somewhere, if not that then there is no shortage of harmonicas or their players. You'd be blown away to see how laid back and earthy we are, should have kept my hair long but the image is made up by the donated clothes.

Picking up all sorts of new words – could write a story with them, i.e.: Francesca and I are taking a vacation, we take showers, tell people to 'grab a brain' and 'get outta here'. It's now 'fall' and it's as cold as a 'refrigerator', the 'garbage cans' have been emptied into 'the trunk' but the 'hood' was already filled with 'motor' that runs on 'gas'. The 'station wagon' had to be traded in for a 'pick up' (or was it a 'truck'?) but even that has an 'attitude' and won't handle the 'highways', it just about makes it 'downtown' but is attracted by the 'sidewalk' which can be a bit risky.

Could go on but I've had enough and I'm sure you have too.

Work last night was gross as somebody had puked in one of the bars and somebody else had had a disaster on the washroom floor in the shopping mall – mmm!

The boss had a night off last night so a whole load of us spent hours being flung around by the floor polisher before learning how to use it – (the boss usually uses the polisher) – big machine!

I now get to drive the truck at work – makes me feel really important. And also I'm one of the longest working members which means I get to tell people what to do and show them round etc. –

what – you could almost call me an exec!

I'm knackered but having a great time and am looking after myself – tons more news, fill you in later. Going up to Lake Louise this weekend with a couple of friends – should be fun as there are some really good hikes and glaciers to see.

Have just realized the date and the fact that you're going away on holiday tomorrow so won't get this until you get back – also Grandma will be at Black Dub and her PC at the cottage. Jen and Robert will also be away, as will Christian – PCs all sent to the wrong places.

Well, I'm about to phone you to say goodbye and have a good holiday – this will probably annoy you owing to the fact that its 5.10am in Britain at the moment! Off to do my vacuuming now.

All love to you all,

Kate

It was time to move on. They drove to Regina and Winnipeg, and crossed into America via 200 miles of Drift Prairie. Kate was asleep and she woke when the car stopped. Francesca told her they'd run out of petrol. It was the middle of the night. At some stage during the hours of darkness, a truck drove up and the driver, far from raping or murdering them, offered to help; he was carrying several spare gallons of petrol and filled the tank. Talk about a good Samaritan.

They drove to Chicago where they stayed for three days. Chicago was the only place where in certain areas they felt they shouldn't stop the car, for fear of vandalism or worse. They actually paid to put the old junk heap in a garage. They took the canary yellow banger on to Washington DC, Virginia, up to New York where they visited museums, galleries, and Boston. Then they ploughed on to Quebec City and Montreal. Finally it was back to Toronto where the car died. It owed them nothing after many thousands of miles.

28 August 1987

Dear Mummy, Daddy, Christian and Ruth

Really had the chance to appreciate the scenery driving through the Rockies, and the wide open spaces of the prairies, hopping through 'Medicine Hat, Moose Jaw, Swift Current, Indian Hat' and

Early Life

Calgary.

all sorts of other bizarrely named places at a rate of knots, and the first place we'll probably spend a few nights in is Chicago if we ever make it over the border.

Really missing my clothes now and am in desperate need of a haircut – one guy quoted me $30.80 saying 'but I'm a European hair-stylist'. Gimme a break, you don't see the average 'June's Hair Stylist' or 'Ken's Hair Care' in Carlisle charging that for a quick clip.

My shoes are now the most violent weapon I possess having been worn every day of the trip. I have to wear 'Beware corrosive gases' and 'Radioactive' signs even if I just leave my laces undone. Can get quite embarrassing staying in youth hostels with twenty to a room – though most people seem to have some sort of gross affliction. The amount of trainers you see hanging on window ledges in these places is incredible, and a lot of people (especially Aussies) have some fear of wearing deodorant! (I tell a lie – I forgot the women who have hair in every place you care to mention!)

Was diddled out of $200 on my last pay cheque. Cheesie and I have been grouchy all day and are sick of being (in the usual hostel manner) sickeningly friendly to everyone.

As we're on our homeward trip we've been thinking of all the home comforts we've missed – proper beds with sheets and pillows, baths, clothes, FOOD that doesn't come out of a packet and is ready in five minutes with just a cup of water and a tablespoon of marg added! Being able to be rude to people you've just had time to discover you don't like, etc., etc.!

Chicago was hot but windy, saw a bear in Banff, went riding today, had my hair cut, farm where we're staying – in Virginia – has ducks, geese, hens and goats, horses, dogs and cats running all over the place. It's very hot, very dry, very dusty. Real Waltons' house with rocking chair on porch and squeaky fly door. Drinking goats' milk and washing with home made soap. All very wacky.

Hope you had a wonderful holiday (but didn't get brown)! See you in a month, roast beef and Yorkshire pud to you all and a little bit of saliva at the same time.

And masses of love, your jet set daughter,

Kate

The girls flew home and that was the start of Kate's passion for travel. We were thrilled to see her, Patrick marginally less so, when she appeared to have had her head almost shaved. The long, wild, curly hair she had fought with for so long, was no more. In place was a boyish crop which showed off her cheekbones. I thought it was stunning.

2

FAMILY HISTORY

To understand Kate's background and the genes that contributed to shaping and determining her life, I have compiled a brief selective family history. With few exceptions I knew all the close family members mentioned, even though they go back to the late nineteenth century, and the family was the biggest influence on Kate, for better or worse.

Patrick and I met at a party in Cumbria when I was sixteen and still at school, and he was 21. He had completed his National Service secure in the knowledge that he had a job to go back to in the family firm, Cavaghan and Gray, in Carlisle. His maternal grandfather had founded it in 1912, as a bacon curing and pig farming enterprise. In the 1960s they had started to develop chilled recipe dishes for Marks & Spencer which they continue to do today. In the 1990s they were taken over by Northern Foods, who also supply Marks & Spencer.

Patrick's father, Frank, ran the family seed business in Carlisle and at the outbreak of the Second World War he volunteered for military service in the RAF air sea rescue. He volunteered at the outset because he wanted to join a part of the service in which he had a particular interest, i.e. boats and engines. Sadly he was killed at Dieppe in 1942 when Patrick was only three years old.

His father's death had a profound effect on Patrick, in part because he felt unable to talk about him to his mother, Dorothy. She did nothing to encourage him to do so. In fact her life stopped when Frank was killed. She married again eleven years later, desperately wanting another child. The marriage was a disaster, but Dorothy did have a longed for daughter, Tana.

As a direct result of Frank's death the decision was made by an uncle, his mother's brother, that Patrick, aged five, should be sent to board at a prep school in order to avoid Dorothy spoiling him; it was traumatic. His teddy bear was fair game in a dormitory of older boys. Initially he was dragged, screaming, from his mother on his return to school after holidays. He did eventually settle in.

For my part, born in 1944 I am the middle child of a wartime marriage, which was destined to be unhappy. My parents were from wholly diverse backgrounds. In spite of relatively modest origins my father was public school educated. His father was headmaster of a private school which he owned and died before I was born.

My paternal grandmother was a complete enigma to me. We rarely saw her as she had moved from Shropshire to North Wales and it was quite a hike, living the Service life that we did then; my father never encouraged much visiting. I had no empathy with her whatsoever. I thought this tall, gaunt, rather austere person very strange. In talking to people who knew them, I learned that they had spoiled my father, their only child, whom they worshipped. Tony, as my father was known, was very spirited, with strong opinions and quite reckless. Early in his RAF career he had taken a plane without permission and performed aeronautical acrobatics.

My mother's family was very much more familiar to me, as we children spent holidays, along with our cousins, at my grandparent's house near Keswick, Cumbria. My brother, sister and I were born there. My mother's antecedents were a banking family who had lived in the Kendal area in Westmorland, now Cumbria, for hundreds of years. Until the late nineteenth century they were Quakers, long established with a very strong work ethic and missionary instinct.

My grandfather, Arthur Wakefield, the youngest of seven children, volunteered in 1900 to serve with the Corps of Sharpshooters in the South African War. Volunteers for the Imperial Yeomanry were usually comfortable 'in the saddle', which he was, sailing to South Africa with his own horse from home in Kendal. He was a medical student at the time.

Arthur studied at Trinity College, Cambridge, and the London Hospital, at each of which he achieved a reputation for all round sportsmanship, particularly in rugby football, fencing, rowing (College boat was head of river), swimming, boxing and cycling in which he was awarded his half blue. He played water polo for the United Hospitals' Team and studied opthalmics at Heidelberg. He held the record for the Fell Walk from 1905 until 1920.

In 1908 he joined Dr Wilfred Grenfell, founder of the Mission for Deep Sea Fishermen, setting up medical missions on the coast of Labrador, Canada. He took with him his new wife, my grandmother, who helped with amputations, dentistry and any other medical problems endured by the Eskimo and Indian populations. They also had a small team of qualified nurses on hand. They travelled thousands of miles on snow shoes and by sledge pulled by huskies, although my grandfather did experiment with reindeer believing it may be faster but it was so dangerous they abandoned that idea.

While still in Labrador, with the First World War threatening, Arthur recruited 90 men, forming the Legion of Frontiersmen, attached to the Newfoundland Regiment. He financed, trained and armed them himself and sailed for France with them. On the first day of the Battle of the Somme 79 of these men were killed. His experience of the war led to his loss of faith and he never went to church again, although he insisted that his wife and children attend regular services.

Being a passionate alpine climber, he was on the team who, in 1922, made an assault on Everest, reaching 27,300 feet. One of his two older sisters, Frances, was among the first women doctors, qualifying in Edinburgh at the end of the nineteenth century. She travelled on her own by ship to North Africa, where she worked as a missionary translating parts of the Old and New Testaments for a local Muslim population. She worked as a medical missionary in Serbia, Egypt, Nigeria and Iraq.

Arthur's eldest brother, Edward, designed and built the first plane to take off from water in 1911. It was flight-tested on Windermere and was the forerunner of the seaplane; Winston Churchill backed the venture as he could see the strategic benefit of something that could take off from and land on water. This became the foundation of the Fleet Air Arm.

I can see the resilience, resourcefulness, generosity of spirit, optimism, exuberance and sheer bloody mindedness running through generations to Kate, and indeed to our two other daughters, Christian and Ruth.

My grandmother Marjorie Younger and her five siblings graduated from McGill University in Montreal, Canada, at the end of the nineteenth century. Their father, James Younger, was a member of the brewing family in Scotland, but chose to leave, settling first in Texas where he owned a ranch and then Montreal where he because treasurer of the Imperial Tobacco company.

My grandmother, Marjorie, was very much in love with a young man, and he with her, while both living in Montreal. She was forbidden by her parents to marry him as they were cousins. Marjorie, or Madge as she was often referred to, then met Arthur Wakefield. There was no objection to their marriage in 1908, although he too was a second cousin. Her parents subsequently allowed a younger sister to marry Madge's first love. One can only imagine how my grandmother must have felt, but – generous of spirit as she was, with no malice – she went about her new life with enormous zest and determination.

My mother was born in 1917 and christened Elizabeth. When of age she changed her name to Anne to avoid being reduced to Betty. It always amused me that she chose to call me Elizabeth. She grew up in an intellectually and politically challenging household where much was expected by Arthur of each member of the family. They lived by Christian principles.

Anne was used to her father, to whom she was devoted, being away for lengthy periods on climbing expeditions. He left instructions with my grandmother that the children's activities in the holidays – by now they were all away at school – had to be educational and written up in diary form. Fortunately his wife had a great sense of fun and adventure and was very sociable so they all managed to enjoy themselves in his absence.

Arthur was adored and admired by his patients when he practised as a doctor, loved and respected by his many friends. He had a forthright and uncomplicated personality. His philosophy of life was composed of a few profoundly held beliefs; in his religion, in his country and his work – whatever he did, he did with the utmost enthusiasm and expenditure of energy. His friendliness was unusually warm and attractive, but his reaction against cowardice, selfishness or meanness was vehement and lasting.

He was very hard on his family. My mother and her brothers were brought up in a tough school with cold baths or a swim in Derwent-water early in the morning, lights out even for my grandmother at 10pm. Anyone not home by then was locked out. Walking the fells, with sometimes reluctant guests, was obligatory. It was a teetotal household, but my grandmother, who loved her gin, knew where some was when needed. Expectations were high, sloth and disloyalty

Kate, Minnie, Ruth and Tiger.

unforgivable. Compassion was a key component in this tightly run household, but all staff, family and guests were made aware if they did not measure up to Arthur's strong principles and code of conduct.

Anne did not disappoint her parents. She was extremely sporty, academic, with a keen intellect and very attractive, tall and slender with a 22 inch waist – not uncommon then. There were distinct resemblances to Kate. She was also very determined and strong willed.

When Anne left school her father was keen that she should go to university. She managed to persuade him that she wanted to become a fashion journalist and so she went to the Sorbonne in Paris to study. She had become a hugely enthusiastic glider pilot and when home from Paris would spend as much time as possible at Dunstable, her gliding club. During this period, just before the Second World War, she became engaged to an eminently suitable young man, the son of family friends, and a member of the same gliding club.

Her fiancé was killed at the outset of war, prompting my mother to join the Women's Auxiliary Air Force. Initially she was stationed at Catterick in Yorkshire. Her godfather gave her a very powerful motorbike for the to-ing and fro-ing from her parents' house near Keswick. She then went south to work on radar, where she met my father, Tony Hill, who was in the RAF.

He had been much in love with a girl who had married someone else, so both my parents were on the rebound. They had met on only eight occasions when they became engaged, not uncommon in wartime when people learned to live as if there were no tomorrow. Arthur instantly disliked the man who would later become my father.

I was born in 1944 into a family dominated by politics and war which continues to influence me. I feel very strongly that our young, my grandchildren, should know our island's history and be aware of what people gave for us to be here today.

My grandmother, who had lived through two World Wars, had a message of forgiveness while not forgetting the atrocities. My parents' generation could not all be so forgiving. But can one ever make progress without communication which may require a certain willingness to forgive, but not expunge?

I was a sickly baby and had pneumonia twice when I was very small. My grandfather, in whose house we were living, put me on to penicillin, one of the first babies to be given this miracle drug. I also had mastoids and a collapsed lung. As a result I think I became a bit of a prima donna and developed quite a temper when I didn't get my own way. With my siblings and our cousins there was some quite brutal teasing and, when I look back I know I did not take it well. My reaction was explosive, on one occasion almost knocking my sister unconscious. We are now the best of friends, but I was not an easy child. I remember being jealous when I felt my older brother Anthony and younger sister Jen were closer to each other than I was to them. My mother used to say I was the jam in the sandwich.

In 1947 my parents, Anthony, Jen and I left England for Australia, where we lived for two years, sailing from Southampton. My Wakefield grandparents travelled with us from Keswick to see us off, my grandfather telling my grandmother that there must always be enough money available to bring Anne and the children home if necessary, as he had serious concerns about my father. Sadly Arthur died in 1949 while we were still in Australia.

His concerns about Tony were justified. He was already addicted to gambling and living close to a racecourse outside Brisbane for two years did nothing to temper this. He had previously pawned a sapphire and diamond pendant and bracelet, given to my mother by her father for her presentation at court in 1935, and she had made over considerable sums of money to him.

Back home, our early childhood was fun and secure, spending much of our time at our grandparents' house, enjoying probably excessive freedom while our mother and father went from one posting to another around England and Scotland. Our lives were not yet overshadowed by the increasing problems with our parents. Those problems were often exacerbated by alcohol, which was at a premium in the Services and was to prove significant in the following years.

When I was twelve I happily went to boarding school in North Wales, as my parents, brother Anthony and sister Jen left for a posting in America. Anthony had been expelled from his public school and it was thought better for him to go to school in Virginia. My father had become military attaché at the Pentagon, Washington DC. They lived in a lovely old colonial house not far from Arlington, Virginia, where President Kennedy is buried.

On their return to England, although many had tried to persuade him to stay in the RAF to which he was eminently suited, my father had had enough and insisted on retiring, commuting half of his pension. On his retirement we moved to North Cumbria, my first proper introduction to the Carlisle area.

My father was a man with many talents, an artist and entrepreneur, with a genius for credible innovative ideas. However, despite his fertile mind he was unable to see one thing through before he was on to the next, and the one after that. Without the foot soldiers to keep wheels turning, this butterfly nature – one might call it lack of self-discipline – combined with his compulsive gambling almost destroyed him and the family.

At that stage it had become clear to us children that our parents were deeply unhappy. We pleaded with my mother to leave my father but she felt she had to stay. He drank heavily and became violent; he could equally be very charming. We were quite afraid of him, particularly Jen. Once, while I was on holiday with the family in America, after a major row with him Jen and I locked ourselves in our bedroom for three days, coming out only when he was at work.

I was not so afraid of my father that I would not take him on and did so on several occasions, my temper getting the better of me. I was always forthright which did get me into a certain amount of trouble, especially at school.

I had an enquiring mind and questioned many things, especially religion and authority when it didn't seem logical. I relished sport, tennis and lacrosse in particular, and loved any subject that told a story, religious knowledge, history, English, and Latin, but I was no academic. I left school only ever wanting to be a children's nurse – having accepted I would never make it as a ballet dancer!

My father had a very low opinion of the nursing profession and flatly refused to let me follow that path. He wanted his daughters to stay at home, do secretarial work and look after him. In his view our mother had clearly failed in that respect.

Looking back and talking to family friends, it became clear that my father deeply resented, and came to hate, the fact that his wife was not the subservient woman he thought he had married. There had been a strong chemistry between them which manifested itself less and less. She was too clever, argumentative and independent. He was becoming more and more abusive towards her. It was an explosive mix and one that I would see re-enacted in several of Kate's relationships.

As often happened, my grandmother took a hand in my future. She had connections with Dr Barnardo's and suggested I think about working for them. I wound up, after a spell in Essex, working at one of two special schools run by the charity. The children were what was then known as educationally subnormal, aged between five and twelve. It was challenging, but I loved it. The school was in Ripon, Yorkshire, an hour and a half from Carlisle, so Patrick was able to visit occasionally. During my time in Ripon I returned home several times to help my mother, when she had been assaulted by my father, on one occasion suffering broken ribs; the result of having been pushed down a flight of stairs.

Eventually Patrick persuaded me that we should be married and, although I was very excited at the prospect, I did feel guilty about leaving the children and staff at the school where I had been so very happy. That then is the background and those are the influences on Patrick and me, and therefore on Kate.

3

LONDON LIFE

On Kate's return from Canada, David Hicks asked her whether she could work for them on a salary, putting colour schemes together and working on design. The timing was perfect and she left for London with great excitement; knowing she had Christian there was reassuring for Patrick and me.

She began by staying with kind friends, often on the floor, and occasionally at Jen's place in Chelsea. When it became clear that she was going to stay in London for a while, she decided she needed something more permanent. She answered an advert in *The Times* and found herself viewing a large, sunny maisonette in Beacon Hill, near Holloway. The landlord, Michael, was so keen for her to take the room that he drove her back to Chelsea from Islington. They ended up becoming both flat-mates and great friends.

After a couple of years of north London life, she moved back to Robert and Jen's flat in Chelsea in return for housekeeping. Living just off the Kings Road was a huge magnet for her friends. They used to hang out there, talking endlessly, drinking cup after cup of Earl Grey tea, moving on to wine in the evening and eating terrible precooked meals, as Kate remained at that point unable to boil an egg.

She met Lucy at David Hicks and they quickly became close. After work they regularly ended up at a rather dodgy pub in Vauxhall called the Black Dog. There they were given pool lessons by an actor from early episodes of *Eastenders*. Kate was the better pool player of the two, which Lucy said was just as well because she was not a good loser. Lucy had had several backgammon boards tipped over her for beating her too many times in a row and she had good reason to worry what Kate might have done with a pool cue!

Patrick and I met Lucy when she came home to Black Dub for the first of many weekends in Cumbria. I packed the girls off to London on Sunday nights with roast beef and onion sandwiches for the journey. Kate cried a bit as she often did. Lucy told me later that she was surprised to see this fearless, free spirit so emotional about going back to urban life. She appeared such a sophisticated city girl. Kate certainly fitted seamlessly into London. It offered her a whole new dimension, satisfying her appetite for life at the time, but there was no doubt that home in Cumbria was where her heart lay.

When David Hicks moved to Chiswick, Kate started to have more of a late night social life. She would often spend the evening with Lucy who lived in West London and, while she had her bath prior to bed, Kate would get ready to go clubbing. This meant she was often tired the next day at work and would curl up on the floor of the dark room to sleep. After a while, it seemed to be accepted that if anyone wanted Kate they would come to Lucy who would vet the enquiry and, if it was important enough, wake her!

However, despite occasionally sleeping on the job, she always produced her finished presentations to her own exceptional standards, and on time, even if the designers left supplying her with the designs to the very last minute. Lucy told me later that she spent many late evenings just keeping Kate company as she worked. Sometimes she would let her help, but her standards were so high often it was easier for her to do it herself.

One of the directors at Hicks, when staying with us, remarked that Kate had a huge natural talent for design, and she progressed quickly while

The Hicks office party.

working for the company, designing a carpet for the Connaught Hotel in London and putting together a design for an Arab palace amongst numerous other projects.

She was equally at ease in black tie dress as in PVC shorts, attending bankers' dinners by invitation of friends or going to a rave in a warehouse. She had a love of vintage clothing (before it had become de rigueur) and looked amazing dressed up in sequins and lace. She loved the free-spirited, out-all-night explosion of energy which the rave culture offered when it first appeared. It was perfect for someone who liked dancing as much as she did and, when she wasn't out clubbing, she took classes in contemporary dance.

In spite of her unconventional image, she valued much of our traditional way of life – loyalty, honesty, integrity and fidelity within her relationships. She would come home with boyfriends, all delightful, and Patrick and I enjoyed having our weekends, all too short, with them. One or two had particular appeal to us as parents, but Kate felt that whilst she enjoyed their company, there was no future in a relationship. They were too 'nice' for her and she would wind up being horrid to them; she needed someone to stand up to her, and she was very strong. She didn't date much in Cumbria. She found it quite a an insular place and she preferred to meet people from outside its narrow confines and conventions.

Between the ages of sixteen and 25 Kate would have been more than happy to have these 'nice' boys as good friends – but inevitably it got to a point where a little more commitment from her was requested. The 'niceness' meant it all stopped there and it sometimes led to acrimony. Was that a portent for the future? Where boyfriends were concerned she certainly showed a marked preference for danger and the unknown over stability and convention, perhaps it should have been a warning.

On her fourth attempt, Kate managed to pass her driving test and for her 21st birthday we gave her an old banger. It died pretty quickly and we were persuaded, against our better judgement, to replace it with a secondhand XR2; there ensued a history of accidents over the next two to three years and many insurance claims. Her initials are

Francis and Christian's wedding, July 1989

carved in gateposts and cut in stone around north Cumbria. She was notorious behind the wheel. I was so frightened of her driving that I refused a lift to London with her. However she prevailed and drove very sensibly all the way south, presumably out of respect for me.

There was great excitement in November 1988 when Christian and Francis announced their engagement, to be married the following July. Patrick was thrilled to have a male join the household – even the dogs were all bitches. There was much ribaldry with the girls and it was a very happy time.

Knowing nothing would be done until the last minute as far as clothes went, I told Kate three months in advance that I would pay for whatever she chose to wear and please could she organize it in good time. Three weeks before the wedding she told me she had bought a rather lovely hat and top, and I was grateful and thought no more about it. We had enough excitement over Christian's dress.

Christian and Kate came home from David Hicks a week before the wedding; a friend of Christian's was making the dress, which was beautiful, with the exception of the front panel which had been sent away to be beaded and hadn't come back. On the Tuesday before the big day we had a family discussion – what to do? Christian, completely calm and matter of fact, said if it hadn't arrived by Thursday she would take a train to London and buy a dress. It actually arrived on the morning of the wedding and she was sewn into the dress over lunchtime. She was an example to us all in unflappability.

Not content with that little blip, Kate announced that while she had got this lovely top, from Joseph, and a great hat, she had nothing to wear from the waist down, apart from shoes. At midnight on the eve before the wedding, the entire household of us and the extended family were asked to produce anything that might do. Fortunately everyone was very relaxed, probably due to a good dinner, plenty of wine, and adrenalin flowing, and this provided much entertainment as Kate tried on one ridiculous outfit after another. I forbade trousers and we eventually found a skirt which, when rolled up several times at the waist, actually looked good.

Early in 1990, having got some great contacts through her years at David Hicks, Kate decided to set up her own company, working from home and dividing her time between London and Cumbria. It worked well, and she had commissions for numerous private houses from several of the well-known interior designers – Mary Fox Linton among others. She took over the annexe of Black Dub, which had been vacated when my mother died.

Dividing her time between London and the country suited her perfectly; as soon as she got restless in one place she could go to the other. Fell walking was one of her great loves, which was what she did with friends who came to stay, spending hours putting the world to rights and very often giving a shoulder to cry on. She was an exceptionally good listener, and very compassionate. It was around this time that I really became aware of how much people went to Kate with their problems, ranging from boyfriend issues to full-scale breakdowns and much in between. I would find her on the telephone for hours, counselling one or other friend who was having a bad time.

After she went missing in 2003, one of the recurring themes in the hundreds of letters from friends was gratitude to Kate for how much she had 'helped them', 'just listened' and even 'turned their lives around from a very dark place'.

She always sought out the good in others, and that coupled with the childlike aspect in her character made her vulnerable to

Kate's smile.

some people taking advantage of her compassion. Honest and forthright in her views, she was confident in times of crisis. She didn't know the phrase 'lost cause'. Where there was life there was hope.

A truly unconventional free spirit, who took joy in the simplest things, it was becoming clear that she would follow her own life path and not conform to the expectations of others. Conversely she was also a great homemaker and wherever she found herself, managed to create a warm, inviting atmosphere.

Timekeeping was still a huge mental block; she didn't even consider it until it had almost run out. She was infuriatingly unaware. As one friend said, 'anything up to a couple of days late was the norm'. Brinkmanship was her middle name, as Curly Kate became her

Above, Kate and Poppy, 1993, and below, Christmas 1994, with Charlie.

forename, yet her paperwork was meticulous; filed, cross-referenced, to hand at any given moment, as were all the tools of her trade.

On 12 October 1992 something wonderful happened in the family. Poppy, our first grandchild, was born to Christian and Francis. No one except possibly the parents could have been more thrilled than Kate, who took every available opportunity over the following years to spend time with Poppy, and with Charlie when he arrived in 1994. Her adoration was reciprocated. She was a bundle of fun, a terrible wind-up merchant, and they loved her for it.

Kate was subject to glorious highs, as well as serious lows. In 1991 she was about to plumb one of those depths.

At Easter she brought home a young man whom Patrick instantly disliked, not just because he arrived with two husky dogs uninvited. There was something about his manner that put his back up. He was an attractive-looking chap, but he had an arrogance which made him hard to warm to. There was a darkness about him, something Patrick and I had not encountered before and found unfathomable. Unfortunately it was clear that Kate and he, both very passionate people, had a chemistry between them.

I have always said we must make all the girls' friends welcome, which had not been difficult up to this point. Boyfriends had come and gone over the years, and we had always done our best to make them feel comfortable with us in our home. This was partly pragmatic; we did not know who the girls might choose to marry, if they did at all, and we knew we should make the best of it or we would be the losers. That did not mean compromising on principles.

This young man was an exception and, when his huskies played havoc with local sheep, killing two, Patrick demanded that he leave. The sheep were not ours – they belonged to a local farmer – and we were all too aware how quickly problems could escalate with neighbours. There was no apology.

Sadly on their return to London they stayed together, and it was confirmed by friends of Kate's that their relationship was volatile. They travelled to North Africa together, which Kate did not enjoy, surprising given how interested she was in foreign culture.

That summer we stayed in the Dordogne in an old chateau with quite a houseful, courtesy of Robert, my brother in law. Kate joined us there but, having just left her boyfriend somewhat acrimoniously, was not her usual vibrant self. We tried to persuade her to come home with us to Cumbria, but she had work in London and said she must return.

She and this young man got back together and it became abusive. I visited her in London and on my arrival she showed me a blue lump on the back of her head. She was quite agitated and I can't remember what explanation she gave when I asked about it, but I took her straight to hospital where they x-rayed her and said it was ok – it would eventually disappear.

She later told me he had banged her head deliberately against some wood. I tried to persuade her never to see him again, which I knew was futile even as I was doing it. It was unfortunate that they moved to some extent in the same circles, although Kate thankfully did have different groups of friends.

I spent the next six months, sometimes on the phone for an hour at a time, trying to persuade her to come home. To my horror, I started to receive long abusive phone calls from him until I learnt to put the receiver down. He was a bully, a manipulative controlling ex-heroin-user. I suspect he was a psychopath, but we did not know him for long enough to establish this.

Kate later said that he had damaged his brain taking heroin, which he was off when they met, and unfortunately Kate had convinced herself she could help him and make things better. As I said, there was no such thing as a lost cause to Kate. By the time she acknowledged he would never change, she had become demoralized and he had gone some way in destroying her confidence in herself. He did his level best to take her down with him, but he did not succeed.

Kate had fallen in love with this man, and I certainly would not want to trivialize the situation. Many women, and indeed men, in the same situation, find it difficult to leave an abusive relationship – often because they are too frightened of the consequences. To some extent her path was carved out and she was going to struggle to change what was in her genes.

My mother, also a very strong woman, was in an abusive marriage, often violent, and it can follow that subsequent generations find themselves in the same situation – history repeating itself. Having suffered years of abuse, my mother was then abandoned for another woman. My father effectively destroyed her for many years but, being as strong as she was, she eventually came through. Having witnessed all this as I was growing up, I feared for Kate. With her passionate nature, and with the heart invariably ruling her head, it could be a difficult path. However, on this occasion, thanks to her fundamental strength and joy of life and to the help of family and friends, she regained her vibrancy. She threw herself into her work and plans for the next adventure.

4

SOUTH AMERICA

Much as Kate loved her work, she was unable to do anything for long before restlessness set in. She needed to be on the move, having adventures, exploring new places. In her late twenties by this stage, she showed less and less sign of conforming or indeed settling down. The next project on the horizon was to explore South America. This she proposed to do in the company of Jen's son, her younger cousin and very good friend, Peter.

She planned to be away for several months. Accordingly, and typically, all paperwork, passport information, bank details, insurance, and everything she could think of was filed and left with us to have on hand should it be needed. She made a will and gave Patrick and me power of attorney. She tidied up the annexe and left it immaculate.

In August 1995 they arrived in Quito, Ecuador, where they found lodgings with local families, and set about adjusting to the altitude and learning Spanish. The language is quite different from that spoken in Spain, and they spent several weeks in Quito studying and exploring, making friends with other travellers the while.

September 1995
Dear Mum, Dad and Ruthie
    Well, I made it – just – up Pinchincha and consequently have my doubts about even attempting Cotopaxi, but as the highest active volcano in the world it would be quite an achievement.[1]
    At present in Bânos, three hours south of Quito. A waterfall is gushing down behind me and I have a beer in front – extremely cheap in South America – same price as a juice – I might no longer be a smoker but could become an alcoholic. Slightly wary of eating meat as I saw a cage full of guinea pigs the other day – and they're not

---

1 She subsequently did climb Cotopaxi.

Peter and Kate on summit of Pinchincha, Ecuador.

that big on keeping pets!

Everything very lively in Quito as August is a month of festivities celebrating their independence. Haven't nearly enough clothes with me and have had to give Peter my fleece as his was stolen. Spanish OK but not too fast as I haven't really learnt anything academically for ten years. I find the grammar quite hard to remember but can happily get myself around.

Well, it's now ten days later and reading through the first part I should tell you that I haven't given up smoking yet. It's hard when they are about 40p a packet. Since Bânos I returned to Quito for one week for more Spanish, living with a family to get to grips with the practical – still haven't moved on to tenses but intend to do more in Quito (on my return), and Peru and Bolivia. It's Monday now and I have spent since Friday at an Evangelist mission in the Sierra. One man and his wife set up, and built a church and school for the local children. The classrooms consist of straw huts on stilts – it's totally beautiful. But the religion I can do without – HALLELULYAH – obviously by the spelling I've been deeply Evangelisted.

Peter had met some fellow travellers in Quito who were planning a trip of some weeks up the Amazon. They had invited him to join them. It was to be a 'boys trip', which effectively left Kate to travel on her own. Kate phoned home and told us down a very crackly line about the change of plan. Patrick and I were very concerned, and Kate was a little dismayed. However she had made friends and would have travelling companions when she wanted them. So Peter went exploring the Amazon and Kate continued on to Peru. A few of them decided to move on as a group for a while, splitting up when their interests diverged and coming together again later.

October 1995
Dear Mum, Dad and Ruth
    Have left Quito again and at this moment am in Esmeraldas (North West Ecuador) on the coast; when I arrived last night it turned out to be the biggest festival of the year, music, dancing, Caribbean style in the streets, fireworks and vibrant atmosphere. Came here from Muisne on the bus having taken a boat to Muisne from Cojimies (no roads) – a beautiful trip around the coast in a small boat that

Pelican crew, Peru.

nearly capsized in the waves, and soaked to the bone. Thousands of pelicans, frigate birds, mangrove swamps, banana plantations, coconut trees, etc., etc.

From here it is possible to take a boat to San Lorenzo and from there apparently the most amazing train ride to Ibarra. Ibarra is very close to Otovala, where I'm intending to get some musical instruments for Poppy and Charlie. It's a market town for that whole area of the Andes. The dress there is very traditional and the Otovala Indians look totally unique. The men and women have plaits down to their bums and pork pie hats and traditional costume. From Ibarra I shall go back to Quito and more Spanish.

Thousands of mosquitoes on this week's trip. From El Carmen (the mission, previous letter) I went to Bahia de Caraques, stayed in a total hovel for two nights and left, running, without a square inch that hadn't been mosquitoed, bed bugged, cockroached – even rats in rooms! From Bahia de Caraques I took a bus to Pedernales (lots of buses everywhere, blow up pillow is a joy) and from there (had enough of bus) – they run cattle and cattle trucks up the beach (it's like speedway and used as the main road). I stayed in the tent beside a remote hotel under the palm trees.

Well, I'm rejoining you in the evening of the same day – I left Esmeraldas at 12 and sat on the roof of an open bus for four hours over dirt roads, and I am filthy and brown/red! I am the only gringo in this entire town (Borbon). The whole place is basically a shantytown and that's a glorified description! The people are lovely, but I can't understand a word they say – and they can't me. I seem to draw a lot of attention.

I've just returned from supper (a merienda, local diner) where I drew a crowd of at least 30, all just watching my every movement. Packed in the doorway, scrambling over each other! Anyway, I'm off to San Lorenzo by boat in the morning. No electricity here and I want to save my candles so I'll save other news till next letter.

Miss you all, love to you all,

All love, your extremely dusty daughter, Kate

October 1995

To all Osbornes and Hiltons

Well, after 1½ hours of trying I eventually got through to you for Poppy's birthday. If this gets to you before the 21st Happy Birthday Mum! I'll try and call (but probably reverse charges as it is the same price from here for three minutes as it is for ten nights in a hotel).

On my way to Billcamba (near Loja) in the south of Ecuador – from there to Puira in Peru → Lima, down to Pisco and apparently some great islands with 'inquisitive sea lions and penguins' and all sorts → Nazca and the famous Nazca Lines – hoping to go to the Colca Canyon → Cuzco where I can do a five day trek to lost Inca city of Machu Pichu and train down to Puna on shores of Titikaka. On Titikaka there is Uros, the floating island made of reeds inhabited by the Aymarans who went there to escape the Incas (starting to sound a bit like a travel brochure!) and lots, lots more; please call for more information!

Doing lots of touring around Titikaka before going to Bolivia (by boat) to Copacabana and from there bus to La Paz, highest city in the world, apparently you pour 1mm of beer and it fizzes out of control to eternity.

Big problems with the hydro electric. They take it in turns each day between the new town and the old, and have twelve hours at one time if it doesn't go off – they're building lots of platforms on the roads, I asked what they're for – trams – would you believe ELEC-TRIC trams are supposed to run, in a city with no electricity! I bought a stove which is now bubbling the water for my tea – how civilized. My room has become quite popular since the acquisition....

Itching fiercely as my bed is full of bugs. I'm getting quite paranoid about getting into it. Someone told me yesterday that if you pull the sheets back swiftly you see them all scuttle away – I spent the night trying to catch one until Peter (with whom she'd met up again) told me I was extremely gullible.

I'm thinking of staying out here for a bit longer, which would mean I wouldn't be home for Christmas after all. Things are all seeming a bit rushed, but I'm very wet about having Yule at home.

Anyway, I'll let you know.

Ready to fly over Nasca Lines, Peru.

It wasn't all plain sailing. She was mugged in Peru and her rucksack taken, but after sorting out passport and insurance, did not make a drama out of it. We were enormously grateful to my brother-in-law, Robert, who pulled a few strings at Morgan Grenfell, allowing us to use the diplomatic bag winging its way from London to Lima and vice-versa most days.

In Lima, they were grateful for help from David Beresford Jones, Morgan Grenfell's man in Peru. He really looked after Kate and her companions; hot baths, the first for a long time, Earl Grey tea, even a civilized dinner party. Most important of all, he took Kate to the British Embassy to sort out her passport and visa.

Kate said of all the South American countries she had visited, Peru was the most threatening. It is no doubt ironic that the man who would prove the greatest threat of all to our daughter came from there.

7th November 1995

Dear All

Plans change by the minute – returned to hotel today Wednesday 7 November intending to leave Lima tomorrow – to find Raphael (an Israeli back-packer with whom she had hooked up) back from the doctor with parasites discovered burrowing into his skin and stomach – so we're here till Saturday at least.

I'm now quite independent again, with new passport, visa etc. When I spoke to the British Embassy in Lima and asked if any of my things were likely to be found, the woman answered 'I have worked here for 11 years and never once in that time has any one thing ever been returned' – a real optimist. I am quite upset at the loss of my diary which had turned into a bit of a novel, and my photos and address book – never mind, I'm making up by taking hundreds of pictures with the new camera – it comes everywhere with me.

In Cuzco at the moment, at 3,400 metres, and arriving from sea level we all got altitude sickness. The old lady that runs the hostel

Vilcabamba, 1995

Shepherds, Sillustani, Peru.

sorted us out though with the local remedy – coca leaf tea! It's legal here and you can buy sacks of the stuff – but only legal over 1,800m.

Today has been election day, they have some strange laws around this time – it is totally illegal to buy or sell alcohol three days prior, 100% of the population has to vote and face heavy fines if they don't – and are daubed with ink that can't be washed off (it's impossible) for ten days, to show that they've complied – consequently the town is packed. A lot of people wear traditional costume and llamas and alpacas are everywhere.

Raphael's parasites are evacuating and amoebas seem better and he, Joe and I are preparing to explore the Inca trail in a few days, to Machu Picchu. Charlotte is going on ahead to Rio as she has a flight in two weeks.

From Quito I went down to Vilcabamba and spent two weeks walking the mountains and hired horses for two days trekking – it's beautiful, lots of photos. The second day I went with an American, Richard – we took the ponies where I'm sure Ruthie would have been horrified – practically up rock faces and along some of the narrowest ridges I've ever seen. So much so I got off and walked. We stopped to ponder what we were doing with two horses there – and would we ever be able to get them back down.

I was adopted by a dog all the time in V-Bamba – it slept on my bed, I was sad to leave.

Dogs are vermin in South America, occasionally served up for dinner; this stray must have thought its luck was in when it met Kate.

Visited Sillustani – huge burial chambers from pre-Inca times. Met the others again here in La Paz, we're just back from a four-day trip to a place called Coroica which is in the Yungas, kind of jungly – great to get away from altitude for a bit, did some more walking and saw some amazing wildlife.

Arrived there from what is apparently the most dangerous road

Slingshot lady, Sillustani.

Floating Islands, Uros.

in the world with an average death toll of 240 per year over a 30-
mile stretch. I've never see anything like it. I was sitting at the right
side for all of the views, but the wrong if you're afraid of heights,
sheer drops that you couldn't see the bottom of, and clouds below –
it's basically a gravel track most of the time only wide enough for
one vehicle – it's quite shocking when you go round a bend and come
across a truck.

There were landslides over the road and waterfalls fell into it from
above – incredibly beautiful – unfortunately saw two vehicles at the
bottom of ravines. Ride back was quite funny, caught a truck as the
driver, who of course charged us, assured us we'd get a bus easily
from Yolosa – what a joke – after four hours of trying, spent a very

uncomfortable few hours on the floor of a bus back to La Paz – we were lucky to get that.

Replaced my watch with a digital one that cost 10 Bolivianos – about a pound! It's got time, date, alarm, stopwatch, day, basically everything!

Still in La Paz but planning on looking around Bolivia for a week or two. Am sending home, when I get to a PO, my sleeping back to lighten the load, three brightly coloured hats, for Poppy and Charlie and Ruthie, also a piece of material for you or Christian – they are all antiques.

La Paz is a great city but we got tear-gassed the other day – all the students are protesting about funding and the police seem to indiscriminately CS gas the whole city.

Bolivia is the first country that has 24 hour power – Ecuador seems to have a 6-10 hour power cut every day. Haven't experienced hot water since leaving Quito except for with David (Beresford Jones). Lake Titikaka was beautiful, visited the floating islands from Puno as a base – everything quite hard work at 4000m.

School in Uros.

Rugmaking in Uros.

On her return to Quito, Kate was introduced to Stefan by a mutual Greek friend, who had assured Stefan that he would love her. The attraction was on both sides and they got to know each other over a few weeks – enough to agree to travel to Colombia together, with two other friends.

While still in Quito, Kate and Stefan were in a club late at night. They came to leave, asking for the return of a jumper she had left in the care of the owner and barman. It was nowhere to be seen and Kate was absolutely furious, demanding it back, to no avail. Her sense of injustice got the better of her and she argued furiously with the staff. She was on dangerous ground.

As she and Stefan eventually walked away empty-handed they were followed and quickly overtaken by some men, one of whom stabbed Kate in the face, causing a deep cut below her nose along her lip. It was serious, and Stefan, who did not speak English but communicated where possible in German and a smattering of Spanish, got Kate to the local hospital from where he rang her cousin, Peter, who was asleep at the guest house. Peter arrived quickly, took one look, made enquiries, and discovered there was an American hospital two hours drive away. He organised a car to get them there and Kate was lucky enough to see an American plastic surgeon who sewed her up with thirteen stitches. He did a marvellous job and although she had a scar afterwards it was barely noticeable.

Stefan, Plaza Café, Quito.

Unlike some of her escapades, we came to hear of this fairly quickly because she had to phone for her insurance details. We were horrified. That she'd been stabbed viciously on the top lip over an old

Children, Cazco, Peru, 1995.

jumper was very worrying. Patrick and I were concerned that Kate just wasn't streetwise enough to get by in South America. We tried to get her to come home at once but she was having none of it. She was very reassuring, said she was going to continue with her travels, and was capable of keeping it clean, changing the dressings, etc. To make light of it, she simply said, 'I just won't look quite the same'. As I reluctantly put the phone down, I wondered if she realized how lucky she had been.

There was some consolation. Another aspect of Kate's meticulous planning was to carry a fully comprehensive medical kit, from dressings to her own syringes, super glue and blades she always had on hand for her artwork, and a multitude of other things, most of which at some time or another she was very grateful for.

23rd January 1996

Dear All

Well, I made it up to the Caribbean for Christmas Eve, and was lucky to do that. I'd bought a ticket from the South to North of Colombia despite being told all flights were fully booked until well into January. No flights go direct N-S or E-W, so the route was Ipialis, Cali, Bogotá, Barranquilla – at every airport I was told the flight was full yet at the 11th hour managed to blag a seat – except for Ipialis – the aircraft from there to Cali is only a 14 person one and seeing only 8 people waiting I was sure of a seat – unfortunately (as I was told) the airstrip is not sufficient for a plane to take off with more than 8 unless, with a very agreeable wind, your fingers crossed, and a little heavenly intervention.

I was in Ipialis for another 24 hours. Couldn't get to Barranquilla but arrived on the coast at Carthagena – a beautiful port town 'steeped in history, one of the most interesting towns in South America' as my book says.

Stayed for two days in the old walled city but didn't feel like

Grinding grain.

Caves, Ica Island, Peru.

doing much; coming straight from the fresh mountain air of the Andes and flying through the climatisation, suddenly to disembark into 40° – in fact it took me a good month to find the heat bearable, and I still have to take walks by the sea to cool down. Fortunately there's a strong wind most days by the water, sometimes gale force, like the Mistral in France – here it's La Loca – the mad woman!

The difference from Peru, Bolivia and Ecuador to here is extreme, the people, the language, the architecture, everything, but then I must have seen 2% of what Colombia has to offer. Just 50km inland from here is the Sierra Nevada mountain range with peaks rising to 6,000 metres. Amazonas in the south east and the rest of the country is criss-crossed by Andean ridges, jungle, desert, swamplands, it is amazing to think as I sit here sweating with my fan on full pelt that in just an hour's bus ride I could be freezing my butt off in some mountain.

Unfortunately got dysentery last week (or that's what I and some friends narrowed it down to from our sparse medical literature). For five days and four nights I was miserable. The second night I moved to a more up-market hotel (this one is a flea-ridden, hammock-swinging, gringo dive). I had to pay five times the price – but wow – I had a private bathroom, I appreciated it so much, I had to sleep on the floor by the loo and only used the bedroom the next day! But all good things must come to an end, and that afternoon I was back at the Miraman.

The doctor came to see me on my sick bed. Remarkable men here, their diagnostic skills and curative medicines, he looked at my hands, he looked at my knees and said he thought I'd be better in a couple of days ? What, no temperature check – I was at the time sitting in my 45° room wearing two shirts, my fleece buttoned to the neck, trousers, socks, sheet and blanket – and I was still cold! – no – nothing else, just my hands and my knees, and of course his bill! Anyway, now I'm feeling much better.

There hasn't been any water all afternoon and probably won't be until tomorrow – joy! But one thing Colombia has that none of the other countries did, is reasonably consistent electricity.

Stefan had become her constant companion. He was to play a pivotal role in Kate's life over the next few years, and indeed still does in life at Black Dub. Born in Switzerland, he spoke German and very little English. When he came over to England this was a source of entertainment, when he became the butt of Black Dub humour. He himself has a great sense of the ridiculous. He is a gentle giant with a lovely smile, and just as stubborn as Kate.

When responding to my question as to how he first communicated with Kate, Stefan replied, 'I call it kind of English speaking. I did, years before when I holidayed in Jamaica, have my first language lessons, and my Spanish is lousy, but, well my English was very basic and rough, Kate did understand/misunderstand (it was entertaining and I learnt fast to choose words carefully)'

Stefan had tried to improve his English when they were in Santa Marta because he wanted to impress Kate at this early stage in their relationship. He told me that once as he walked behind her he said something which he hoped meant 'I like the way you move' but judging by Kate's reaction must have been more along the lines of 'you've got a fat arse and bendy legs'. By the time he had gone through a long explanation, the sexiness of the moment was gone.

Sunset Taganga, 1996.

English may not have been Stefan's strong point, but he came into his own when Kate became sick. Although they were only a couple of weeks into their relationship, he looked after her, even carrying her around in his arms when she was too weak to move. He couldn't believe that this 'goddam goddess' as he referred to her was so violently throwing up. He patiently negotiated with Kate when she refused to allow the doctor into the room, 'Not an easy task for me to do that day'. I don't think Stefan knew quite what had hit him.

To repay him for his nursing, when Kate returned to health she invited him to a fancy restaurant for their Christmas celebration. Stefan misread the menu and ordered what he thought would be a delicious dinner of fish and vegetables but in fact turned out to be a local delicacy involving large squid and ugly sea slugs. When he started to pick at it mournfully, Kate with great kindness and in order to keep the peace, just swapped the plates and tucked into the seafood dish as though it were just what she had hoped for.

After two months in Colombia the little group, Miguel, Chiara, Richard, and Jim, accompanied Kate and Stefan by boat across the Canal to Panama, and by bus to Honduras, exploring wherever they could. On their boat crossing the Panama Canal they had the best and biggest English breakfast ever, but were then all sick!

They found their way to Costa Rica and Nicaragua, and then returned to Bogotá from where they flew home.

Stefan said Kate was the best travelling companion; she knew her way round all forms of transport, where best to sit to get some sleep, how to negotiate the most advantageous terms, source the freshest food, and all-in-all entirely practical on day-to-day existence.

But for now they had to think about more mundane things. They were returning home having come to know each other and feeling they would like to continue their relationship. It would be interesting to see how they would cope within the confines of the Western way of life, very different from the laissez faire lifestyle they had enjoyed over the past few months.

5

HOME AND SWITZERLAND

It was April 1996 when Kate returned – for us it had been a long nine months and her first Christmas away. Her homecoming was joyful, exciting – just wonderful to have her back. She was such a great hugger; I can still feel the warmth of them. Patrick and I were delighted to see that the American surgeon had done a good job. The scar was almost invisible.

It was going to be more difficult for her to continue her design work solely from Cumbria, although not impossible. She embarked on a computer course in Carlisle and a correspondence course on the art of writing – though having received hundreds of letters from her over the years I'm not sure she had much to learn on that front. To augment her income she announced that she had decided to take up taxi driving in Carlisle. She was going to do what? Patrick made her repeat it several times as the full horror of what she was proposing sank in, but it wasn't a joke. Kate had decided that being a cabbie was a good honest way to make a living. We were very concerned about this. Driving had never been her forté; she'd had numerous scrapes over the years, as our insurance claims testified. We were relieved when it didn't last too long, finishing when she had one too many encounters with difficult situations at night.

She also indulged another great interest when she became informally apprenticed to a young cabinet-maker, learning to make rustic furniture. We were proud to have some pieces and felt she could have made a living from it as she proved she had a natural talent. She made a particularly attractive small oak table, with beautifully carved initials, which we have in one of the bedrooms. It was all going rather well except that the cabinet-maker's mother was making more of it than Kate was happy with and made her feel uncomfortable. Kate, always sensitive to atmosphere, backed out of the situation. It clearly wasn't going to be her next career move, although from then on she was always knocking up something useful from timber lying around at home.

The neighbours! Carrock Fell behind Black Dub.

Being an aunt meant the world to Kate. As much time as she could find was spent with Christian, Francis, Poppy (four) and Charlie (two), all now living in Cumbria. Kate loved them being so close by and adored playing with them in the garden, messing about with balls and cricket bats, giving them piggybacks and swinging them around; then there was Ruth. Although there were eight and a half years between them, these two were the unmarried sisters and very close.

Kate and Ruth enjoyed a good social life as there were quite a lot of people of their age around. There were the usual parties and pubs to go to and Ruth was more than happy to show off her globetrotting big sister. They raised a fair amount of cain together. I often felt Ruth at 20 was more mature than Kate, who at 28 still portrayed that child-like quality which would manifest itself throughout her life.

Kate and Stefan, the man she had met in Ecuador, wanted to continue their relationship, but given the logistics, he in Switzerland and she in England, it was going to be testing. There was also the small matter of each earning a living.

In the summer of 1996, it finally came to pass that this man whom we had heard so much about, came to stay with us at Black Dub. Kate met him at Newcastle Airport. He was so nervous of meeting us – and I think there were some nerves on her part too – that they put in some time at a pub on the way home for Dutch courage. He spoke little English except for the scraps she was teaching him, which were often misleading, causing much laughter. She translated quite naughtily. Language barrier aside, Stefan had a lovely presence, he smiled a lot, and first impressions were good. We'd seen a lot of boyfriends come and go but right from the start he seemed different. Of course he met Ruth, Christian, Francis, Poppy and Charlie with whom he became, and remains, firm friends. He was a natural with the children, who loved him.

Stefan had never been to Britain before and Kate wanted him to see what she considered to be the most stunning places. They walked all the local fells, and the north and western lakes, going from one valley to the next via the wonderful dramatic passes, Hardknot, Honister, Wrynose, Kirkstone, visiting Grizedale Forest and the sculptures. Kate took him to the places she knew well as a child, the house where my brother and sister and I were born and spent our childhood, and the village where the three girls had spent a lot of their earliest years with my grandmother after she downsized from the big house.

Later in the year Kate drove to Switzerland for a reciprocal visit. On her first visit to his country Stefan introduced her to his friends and took her to some of his beautiful places. She took stunning photographs of snow-capped mountains – from Kandersteg she photographed the Oeschinensee and there are wonderful shots of Interlaken, the Eiger, Breithorn and Kiental which she took from Niesen. They stayed with his friend Gertrude in a lovely old wooden house in the country near Wimmis. This visit was relatively brief as Kate was anxious to continue her computer and writing courses, and there was some design work in the pipeline.

Stefan joined us for Christmas at Black Dub that year and proved to be the easiest person to have to stay: helpful, yet unobtrusive, he would take himself off to play his guitar if he felt the need, and rather

Top, Peters Grat, Breithorn, Switzerland, 1996 and below, Stef, Kate and Nico, Oeschinensee, Switzerland, 1996.

importantly he was extremely good with my mother-in-law who liked attention. He opened up more on this visit, alluding to a very difficult childhood after his father committed suicide. For such a warm-hearted person, he had dealt with a great deal of pain in his life. When he met Kate he had been at an incredibly low point. He confessed he felt, 'Too ugly for this gorgeous girl to fall in love with.'

There was something about his quiet charm and big smile that communicated volumes in spite of the language barrier; he also proved

Oeschinensee, Switzerland.

.

himself to be an exceptionally good cook, great at keeping log baskets full, and mending anything in need of repair, and at our home there is always something. Both he and Kate had frugal living down to a fine art. Our attic is still stuffed with bags of materials Kate absolutely forbade me to throw out, including my old maternity clothes, and whenever she was home she would rummage through them to find fabric to make up to augment her wardrobe. She had become more exotic in her dress by this stage, often wearing colourful Indian cotton

Stef at Black Dub, Christmas, wearing leather trousers he had made.

tops with loose Thai fishermen's trousers. It was her personal rebellion against the power dressing of the 1990s and with her height, slim frame and long hair it was a look she could carry off well.

I remember Stefan staying with us on one occasion and making himself a pair of leather trousers, which he was actually able to wear. Needless to say he was soon taking orders from the family!

At the end of 1997 Kate made a lengthier trip to Switzerland.

Dear Chris (Christian) -
Sorry about the drab card, the only nice one cost £3 can you believe so you've ended up with 'Bellisima!' Your present is in London at Miranda's along with the kids' Easter things but Ma says no one is going down. I'll try and get her to send Easter things as they're light but think your pressie will have to wait until April.

We're both coming over for the wedding (Kate's cousin Peter was marrying a girl he had met in Ecuador) and I think will drive up on Friday. I don't have any clothes with me so warn Ma that she'll have to dig some things out for me. I don't know whether I'll be coming back here after – I want to finish my computer course – which will help enormously with the writing course – we'll see.

Anyway, I haven't got much more news, things are going well, though Stefan hates his job, but the quality of life for people here is twice that of England.

See you all in April. Until then all love to you all and Happy Birthday. Hello Poppy, hello Charlie. Kate.

Dear All,
It's Friday, Stefan should be home about 4pm but we don't have anything planned for the weekend. We've spent the last week, or rather I have, decorating our new room; we were living in Marcel's house – he's in Thailand – it's on three floors. On the ground floor is a bar run by Meccu and Marcel – more a speakeasy really and thankfully only open three days a week – then there's the middle floor, kitchen, bathroom, office and two bedrooms – we have the top floor, a lovely attic room, quite big with a huge ceramic stove which Stefan fixed a couple of days ago.

I brought out lots of my Indian sheets so it now looks more like a Bedouin tent, and have managed for only £100 and a little help from

Ikea and the 'Brockenstubes' (second hand furniture) to kit it all out. I found a lovely old hand-painted chest and two huge Persian rugs just sitting in the attic! Stefan has a monster bed we've put up and we have a great veranda ☺ !

There's an American guy working across the road who comes over for lunch every day. He manages a video distribution company and has a whole stash of English ones – great! Most people seem to speak English which I'm not sure is helpful for my Swiss German – but

Kate at Hasliberg, Switzerland, 1997.

I'm picking bits up slowly, supermarket trips amusing though!

I've found a brilliant bookshop in Bern, only 30 minutes away, and can get anything for you as well as carrying a large stock of English written – a whole floor.

Haven't been cooking so much recently as the freezer got full and everyone got sick of eating my leek and potato or vegetable soup. A lot of the ingredients are hard to find without going to Bern; it's a funny town, as it's so small yet has an Ikea, and a MacDonalds opened last week.

Stefan has taken me to some really beautiful places here. We spend a lot of time touring on the motorbike as the weather is so nice. There's one place about ten minutes away, Lueg, lovely, where you can see the whole of Switzerland from; the Eiger, Jungfrau, Munch, very spectacular, especially early evening on a sunny day. They're snow capped all year and we still have snow sometimes, but more often than not it's sunny whatever the state of whiteness.

Yesterday we went for a four-hour walk from here to Winnigen, on the Planetenweg – Planetway! Someone has put the line of planets, from Pluto to the sun, over the mountains, all to scale, something like 13,000,000 to one! We came back by train which, being Swiss,

Kate and Lucy, Hasliberg, Spring 1997.

ran, to the second, on time.

Still going around on the motorbike a lot although it's needed a few repairs since we let the bed slide down the stairs last week – right out of the front door and straight on to the bike (it was too heavy!). Car is going well but I hardly use it.

All love to all. Hope all's well at home Ruthie.

Write soon,

Kate.

The family, including Stef, at Peter's wedding, 1997.

Kate came home after Peter's wedding and got on with work. Stefan joined her in the summer and they went to the TT races on the Isle of Man, travelling on his motorbike. On their return, not a mile from Black Dub, Kate riding pillion, they failed to take a sharp right hand bend and went into a wall. The bike was a write-off and Kate hurt her back, but they were otherwise unscathed.

'Heroes and Villains' at the Front Page Club, Carlisle,
Christmas 1997.

It was Ruth's 21st in December. As usual this was to be in the barn, a real cross-generational family occasion with all her mates, godparents and old family friends. Again we were grateful to have Stefan visiting. Unknown to us at the time, he went to the local garage in the middle of festivities to buy diesel to refuel the empty generator, which was powering everything from the caterers to lighting and the band. We learnt the hard way that it is essential in a situation like that to have an independent electricity supply.

I was going down with flu at the time of the party, felt really run-down and remember warning the girls that they might have to do it alone. A friend was doing the catering and Kate was quite happy being left to her own devices in decorating the barn. I went to the doctor, explained how dreadful I felt and could he give me something to tide me over? Well he did and somehow I made it through the party itself, but the following day I succumbed, adrenalin having kept me going up to that point. In the days after I had a pretty total collapse. I remember lying on the floor barely able to get up. Everything was in pain – sternum, pelvic bones, shins, collar bones – from my head to my feet – it's difficult to describe how terrible I felt.

The doctor said I'd got flu pretty badly and prescribed loads of pills including valium. Everything was becoming a blur. When my speech started to go and I could no longer string a sentence together, he suggested I go to the hospital in Newcastle for further tests all of which came back negative. I continued to get worse instead of better. On one occasion when I was in the surgery having yet another blood test, I overheard one of the nurses saying something about ME. I like the bottom line, so I questioned her about what she'd meant. 'Hasn't the doctor told you?' came the reply.

The doctor confirmed that I'd had flu so badly it had turned into Myalgic Encephalomyelitis or ME. On one hand I was pleased it was not a rare wasting disease, but on the other I wasn't sure that I could identify with a diagnosis of chronic fatigue. Wasn't that something that happened to more delicate people? I was always extremely energetic, working with the horses, eventing, being a wife, mother and grandmother and running the home. I didn't see myself as the fragile type. Having given myself a moment to take in the news, I said I was most worried about my speech which had continued to deteriorate. He said that ME can affect the brain in that way, but that it would come back.

For six months I couldn't go anywhere. I couldn't put on the kettle, lift a plate or cross the yard. I spent most of my time in bed. I couldn't bear to be touched. After several months, the acute pain started to ease. It was a very gradual process of recovery. I tried all sorts of homeopathic potions with varying degrees of success. As I was getting better and able to do a bit more, my body would tell me that I was going brain dead and should go and lie down. It took months to wean me off the many pills I'd been prescribed.

I had been a keen tennis player before. For at least a year I couldn't even hold a racket. Four years later I was playing again – it took me that long to return to fitness and I was lucky compared to many.

After some months, during which the family were absolutely wonderful and supportive and I was lucky enough to have a brilliant GP, Kate, ever forthright, said, 'Mum – could it be a case of mind over matter?' It wasn't hurled at me or intended as a criticism and I wasn't offended; in fact I've often smiled about it since, when I remember – the girls will never let me forget – frequently saying as they were growing up 'remember to smile' and 'mind over matter'! Kate and I talked a lot during this time. The house was quiet and she would often come into my bedroom and we would chat for hours.

Nine months after I first went down with the illness, I felt well

New Year's Eve party 'off the stage'.

enough to go to a big drinks party nearby. But perhaps it was too early – old friends came up to greet me and I didn't recognize some of them; I couldn't attach names to faces either. Similarly when I went back to work with the horses, albeit on a more modest scale than before, I had to re-learn basic tasks like putting on stable rugs or assembling tack. It was infuriating, puzzling, but over time I had to accept that these things had gone with a bit of my brain.

I asked Patrick recently what it was like living with me at that time and he just said in his droll way, 'pretty awful'.

6

INDONESIA

In August 1998 Kate decided to travel to Indonesia. The plan was to go for three or four months, visiting as many of the islands as she could. The restlessness had set in again and, although she probably did not recognize it as such, I wonder now if it was becoming something of a spiritual quest.

A pattern was developing as her date for departure approached. She became tense, and for us it was like treading on eggshells. As ever, her planning was absolutely meticulous, she packed and then ruthlessly re-packed, taking only the essentials in her well-worn backpack. Every evening for the week prior to her leaving it was like having the Last Supper, as we worked our way through roast beef, mince, cottage pie, Cumberland sausage, roast chicken, cold meat and baked potatoes, and roast lamb. These were what she would miss most, and you could be forgiven for thinking we were serious carnivores. And then there were the great big hugs and the awful goodbyes, but she was compelled to go, and we had to let her.

Another habit that was developing was her coming to my bedroom about midnight – I would be in bed by 10.30 or so and Kate, who had her own time clock, was never ready to retire until after the witching hour – and gently ask whether I would like to talk? I have always been an extremely light sleeper so took no rousing, and felt I must allow her this time while she was at home – and indeed I wanted it nearly as much as she did; this beautiful complex daughter whom I knew inside out, but did not necessarily understand. So we would sit up drinking cups of tea for anything from one to two hours talking about everything until she lost me.

We talked about Stefan. He'd been over again for a visit in the summer. As ever he had thrown himself into family life at Black Dub – wild games in the garden with Poppy and Charlie involving hosepipes, picnics and ponies. They seemed good together. He had work to do in Switzerland, so he wouldn't be accompanying her on the trip, but that was OK. Kate was perfectly happy travelling by herself. Kate kept her cards close to her chest when it came to relationships.

We often talked about religion during our nightly chats. I came from a fairly Christian background, not institutionalised, and felt the church had much to offer as I still do. But I'm in a minority of one on this. To my regret the girls did not share my convictions. I would have liked us to be more of a church-going family but Patrick was definitely an agnostic and regrettably I did not fight my corner. When the children were little, weekends were family time and I didn't make the time to go on my own. Kate and I discussed the need for spiritual belief – it was something she hankered after too, though she was most drawn to Buddhism. But I didn't believe there was only one right way; it was just the right way for me. I was very open to exploring the idea of religion with her. In fact we went so far as to book a Buddhist retreat together once, but Kate had to cancel at the last minute.

There is no doubt we had 'quality' time together – that dreadful modern expression – time we both needed and valued. Kate was very spiritual, very deep and sometimes on a level I struggled with. She had a questioning intellect and read voraciously: *Women who run with the Wolves*, *Zen and the Art of Motorcycle Maintenance*, and books by Carlos Castaneda. She liked Celtic patterns, West Indian folk tales and the geometric riddles of Escher. The book she turned to again and again though was *The Prophet* by Kahlil Gibran. She read to me once a passage that summed up her sense that our destiny has already been mapped out for us: 'We choose our joys and sorrows long before we experience them.'

Cumbria alternately nurtured her but then stifled her. Now she needed to be free. It was time to go.

After three weeks on Bali, Kate and a friend decided to travel together to some of the other islands which make up the 14,000 plus archipelago. She was with an Australian friend, Paul, whom we had met when he dropped in on Black Dub. Much to her embarrassment,

I remember saying to him, 'Do look after her', as though she was fifteen years old rather than thirty.

Paul, a dedicated surfer, was in search of the perfect wave. As they explored the beaches of Indonesia, he would be pursuing his passion, but they would be able to see some fantastic scenery and get off the beaten track. Kate found she kept bumping into other friends from South American days, so she wasn't short of company. This was always a relief to us, as we were never entirely happy when she travelled alone, which happened often enough.

Dear All   August 1998

I got your two emails three weeks ago – thank you, but things were very hectic and it was the day we left to come here. We're returning to the mainland tomorrow – hence the letter.

Bali was great but really touristy, hundreds of Aussies use it as their Costa del Sol! And it's a real surf haven so not very interesting though beautiful, hot, volcanic, palm-treed and everything. Anyway, while there I based myself in Kuta in a little back street – they call

My hammock, my Indonesian teacher, Toughnut, Anas and Tika.

them 'gangs'. It's like a maze, and after ten days I still haven't orientated myself.

It's not the usual flea-ridden pit I'm used to.

Because the economy is a bit stuffed things are outrageously cheap – a full breakfast for two with juice and coffee is 25p and a three-course supper about a pound. Everything has to be haggled for and it's easy to forget that you're haggling over what are in fact pennies!

I got bitten by a monkey here on my second day – very sweet. I was with it for ages and it climbed up for a cuddle then when I tried to put it down – crunch – it held on for ages. I wanted to hit it but thought it would bite down harder – anyway, all's well and I still have my finger!

The Indonesians are great – always smiling and so much gentler than the South Americans.

Paul – friend – hired a motorbike and everyday we cruised around (usually to different surf spots for him but nonetheless to some beautiful tranquil places). We did a tour of the North taking in volcanoes and waterfalls, the island is so small – and kind of like Ecuador

Tika at my window, September 1998

in that it has everything of Indonesia but compacted. The Aussies never leave the South so it was back to travelling without the catered tourist package.

We met an Aussie guy, David, who told us about this beautiful spot (where we are now) in Sumatra – so a flight to Jakarta (Java), a boat to Padang (West Sumatra), another boat to Siobhan and then a dug out ride through the ocean for a few hours to here, and this is Katiet. I tried to look it up in my *Lonely Planet* – the page, the single page mentioned one of the Mentawai Islands and said of the others – only for the hardened travellers – and that was it – no map of where we are – no nothing. So picture it – a tropical island, 15 hours from the mainland where only two or three white people make it a year. The people in the dug out tried to tell us 'oh no, nowhere exists, no place to stay' (in Indonesian of course, ours very limited then). Eventually we came to a deserted bay, beautiful white sand, blue lagoon, you get the picture! I had felt very stranded on a deserted beach with the rucksacks and a board back! But as often happens in these places, after a short walk, the people found us – the news of strangers travels fast.

The old people can't speak a word of Indonesian, only their local lingo. They look great with filed teeth and tattoos.

We're staying in the house of the man who seems to be the head of the village (i.e. the one that buys everyone's coconuts and makes the copra to sell on (coconut oil), the one who sells everyone the fuel for their lamps, whose children actually went to school (on the mainland) and most importantly the one who has the boat that will take us back to civilization!). Anyway, as I'm sure you can imagine, we've caused a bit of a stir – we can't do anything alone – be it read, put up a hammock, snorkel – whatever – there's an entourage, mostly children. It can get quite annoying if things aren't going well, i.e. the hammocks which we made ourselves, and took a few tumbles to get right – in the blazing heat and with 20 villagers laughing and staring at the crazy westerners!

Having thought I wouldn't bother learning much Indonesian this place has changed it all. I had the idea that any Asian language would be impossible with no similarities or context. Through necessity I opened up my Indonesian book (thank God I brought/bought it!) and it's great – a really simple language – and I now speak way better Indonesian than Spanish – though what use it will be when I leave! I make lots of mistakes ie Kapila (head) Kelapa (coconut) which sets off a few shrieks!

They're such simple people, the smallest things please them. I showed some children snakes and ladders and now everyday for about five each they play, whooping with excitement every time one gets a ladder etc! We leave a hammock and as you're 20 feet away, turn back and there are six people in it. My mask and fins have been borrowed by several teenagers – but they never put the mask on properly and it fills up as soon as they put their head in.

This family has six children ranging from six to 22 and only three rooms in the house. As head of the village he keeps one empty – I think he's expected to put up any visitors from other villages, and us of course! It's beautiful, right on the beach – you can see the surf from the window – it's all wood on stilts and made mostly from the remains of some Aussie boat that sank on the reef, much to their amusement! You do see boats every day, the Mentawais are an elite surf location for the serious wave seeker but they never come ashore. Paul has met a few out on the break but they're full of stories of the malaria (which is the one drawback) – a serious problem here but I'm very careful – it's almost like a vampire movie or something watching the sun getting low and getting back home in time to cover up.

Anyway, the only time you get to yourself – as I've discovered – is when you walk up past the loo area, a small lagoon half a kilometre up the beach – sacred ground and nobody follows you up there – and beyond, two more beautiful lagoons! So generally I've got it pretty sussed. Paul is off surfing, snorkeling, fishing, I have the use of a small one man dug out and I go off swimming, snorkeling, a lot of hours learning Indonesian, chatting to locals, playing with the children, and of course the everyday chores. It takes half the day to do the basics of washing with water from the well.

The bummer of the whole thing is that Paul's visa runs out in ten days and we have to leave tomorrow to get the weekly boat from Siobhan back to Padang. From Padang we're making our way to Malaysia, probably flying from Medan (we have to leave the country to get visa extensions). David told us about this place after staying with Paul for a few weeks before I arrived on Bali. He asked us not to tell anyone

Eric Allyne, Siobahn, September 1998

about it and I won't. It's beautiful like it is and I would hate to come back in five years time and find it spoiled – or someone else staying here!!

Got loads of great photos, and I've lost those bits on the sides of my hips! (a diet of fish and rice!). As I said, we're going to Malaysia and then I hope to come slowly back to Bali, but it's all up in the air so I could be home Oct/Nov.

All my love – thinking of you, Kate

Dear All September 1998

Not much time to write, but another on its way packed with news.

I've sent Ruth a parcel of photos till now – mostly Sipora (the island) and some of Bali – interesting to flick through but I'll tell you about them when I'm home. It also contains two letters to Ruth (sorry – personal!!) and details if she wants to come out.

This is very hurried as we're leaving here – last minute decision – to go to Singapore. Our visas are about to run out and we have to leave the country to get new stamps – we decided Singapore would be better than Malaysia (closer and cheaper), so we're flying to Pulau

Batam and catching a boat, staying for one night then back to Sumatra. I'm going to Medan in North Sumatra to Lake Toba (Danau
Toba) – Beristagi and to an Oranghutan sanctuary at Bukit Lawang
(Orang in Indonesian is person and hutan means forest) – interesting
huh!

My Indonesian is coming on a treat – I've been teaching myself
and spent hours a day at it on Sipora. Good way to pass the evening
hours with a paraffin lamp! Anyway, I out-learned my phrasebook
etc. over there and have invested in a dictionary and a language book.
Can you believe I'm actually enjoying it? It's a very simple language
that everyone speaks besides their local languages and is also used
in Malaysia and I think (hope!!) Singapore. Anyway, it has no con-
jugations and only three words for past, present and future. Though
a little more complicated than that, that is really how it works – yeah,

Anas and Bumphead, September 1998

suits me!

I know it's ok to tell you I'm travelling on my own for a while as by the time you get this I'll have met up again with friends. As I said in Ruth's letter, this is the safest place I've ever been, so friendly and laid back, and no reports of any stealing or anything.

Better go and eat and pack – early start. Hope you're all well and Charlie's haircut is growing out!" (Poppy had taken the scissors to Charlie's hair!)

All my love, Kate.

Dear All   September 1998

So we scrubbed up before hitting the big city, so strange seeing it rising off the horizon, English speaking, everything available, thoroughly modern Singapore. We were in such spaced-out moods from our time in Mentawai, it was all a bit of a shock and we weren't really interested in seeing the city – but the supermarket's a different matter, wine, cheese, fresh milk, even Carr's water biscuits and Marmite!

We spent two hours trailing every aisle, 'Wow' and 'Hey, check it out' as we called to each other on our discoveries. Then back to our hotel where we ate (and drank) the night away! Fish and rice on the island for breakfast, lunch, and supper had got a bit much – the alternative to fish – an egg! But better than the tuna that was caught three days before we left (and looked like it would last another three after!). It has such a pungent taste – I'll never eat it again, and all in the same sauce – I think to preserve it?

Back to Singapore though – we lasted one night.

I headed on my own to Medan and on to an orangutan rehab centre in the jungle to the north of there, a beautiful place, a village set around a fast flowing, big volume white water river – the only way into the reserve in a dug out across the squall. There the sick primates are kept – most of which have fallen out of trees! Sounds like a fish drowning, huh! Then from there; trails through the jungle – I arrived at an unappointed time – and went wandering, not really sure where to – a little nervous in my unfamiliar surroundings, and came across two wardens at feeding time, with the great apes appearing through the trees, to get their fill of bananas and wash. Most of the animals there had been rescued and released but stayed in the area.

One, Minna, who is apparently very vicious, has attacked more than 50 unsuspecting people on jungle wanders, what a thought, being bitten by an orangutan – the jaws on them! And then all the rabies jabs needed – urgh. She has such a dislike for strangers that they warned me to look overhead as she has a habit of relieving herself on the unobservant. She tried. And missed!

On the walk back to the camp, with all the notes fresh in my head (and the memory of my monkey bite from Bali) I was very alert, an orangutan was following me through the trees, and without warning was at my feet and climbing aboard (sounds dodgy – climbing up). I froze 'Oh God, please don't bite me'. The warden was there, prized him off, me a static statue. If only I'd known it wasn't Minna but Johnny, a seven year old, very affectionate who just likes a cuddle and carry every now and then. What a shame I didn't know, a rare chance for such contact – never mind. Back in the centre I spoke to one of the helpers who told me all about Johnny's antics – stealing tourists cameras, posing for photos, literally for each shot. He mimics you and has little dances he does with the wardens. He helps with the washing, climbs into the buckets and stamps around on the clothes.

From there, back to Medan, I'd intended to go to a huge lake but by then I knew Ruth was coming and thought we could go together, so I headed out to Nias to meet up with Paul. In Medan, trying to organize my transport, I met a great guy, Mike, from South Africa, headed in the same direction – me having spent two days trying to sort out a means, he turned up and jumped on my plans – great for him – on a three week holiday from work in Bangkok – he wouldn't have had time to spend.

Nias, another island off the West of Sumatra, but more north than the Mentawais. Here is so strange, all the same country, but an archipelago – I don't know how many islands – millions! Nias doesn't have a great deal to offer, some interesting villages BUT (for Paul) an amazing wave, reasonably inaccessible, not for the faint hearted surfer – so good they have an international surf competition there – and that's Lagundri Bay – so there I am, a surfers paradise, but, b... all for anyone else! Time to learn – mmm! Several half drownings,

Kate and Anas, September 1998

lots of bruises and quite a few coral lacerations later – and still a crap surfer – thank God for my Frisbee, a ping pong table, binoculars (to watch the good surfers etc) and some great people.

My time in Nias was cut short by the crazy Niasens; for centuries they have been warring tribes and I suppose that's in their psyche because for sure they're psycho. It started with a little trouble we heard through the locals – a few fights but all centred in Teluk Dalam (a village 4-5 km from Lagundri). Then it started getting worse, one man had lost his arm to a machete! The next day we saw Teluk Dalam burning – the smoke rising from behind the hill, that afternoon the ash was falling from the skies in Lagundri – not so pleasant when we're told five had died – three with machetes and two burned alive! – so the ash?

After my experiences in South America I was feeling quite nervous – stuck in Lagundri which is the end of the road – the only way out, back through Teluk Dalam, but was assured by everyone – no problem here, it stays there. So off we went for supper. Sitting in a restaurant with Mike and Paul, another couple there, an English girl and an Indo guy. Obviously there was something going on, all the Indos chatting, and the English girl explaining maybe it wasn't so good to be there (a Chinese owner – the victims if there's trouble to be had). Suddenly her boyfriend grabbed her 'Time to go'. I looked around, motorbikes flew into the entrance, machetes and helmets galore.

I shot up, headed for the loo, before a guy grabbed me saying 'this way'. Out of the back, onto the beach, all the electricity cut off, running through the dark and into somebody's bungalow. Two Japanese blokes who hadn't a clue what was going on – me still terrified, trying to wipe the tears from my cheeks before anyone saw in the candlelight! I hadn't realized how much past experiences had stayed with me until then. We waited for an hour, the Japanese, Paul, Mike, the guy who helped me, trying to hear in the dark. Paul and another – gung ho – crept back to the restaurant to see what was happening – darkness, and only the sound of hurried packing (or maybe looters?) That night they torched some houses in Lagundri and all of us travellers spent our time together (ten or fifteen of us) plus Mike and one other and I started making plans to leave. We organized a van to take us through Teluk Dalam and back to Gunung Sitoli – the only entry point into Nias. The next day at 12 o'clock he'd meet us – and we waited and we waited, the phones down. The electricity cut off, and now no traffic coming through.

Thankfully the other guy was on the case – he found some kamikaze nutter who was willing to make the run, on an old road through the mountains that is left to the elements, as the rainy season is too much for the economy to handle. We set off, with our driver, his machetes – and a couple of his friends and theirs, and three revved up travellers! We found out why the road has been left to its own devices, and with double the amount of time needed for the coast road, and a few hair raising hours later, made it to Gunung Sitoli. Mike and I on to a boat to Sibolega (Sumatra) and Andy, the other guy, lucky b… with a flight to Medan.

We got back to the mainland and chartered a car to Medan, a lovely drive, if long, across Sumatra, spent 24 hours enjoying civilization and MacDonalds before Mike headed for Malaysia and I to Bali. Beautiful Bali! I had such a wind down after Nias, met an Aussie on the plane who I spent a couple of days with, and all the old friends from Bali and Paul followed a few days later.

Ruth had been talked into visiting her big sister on Bali following the end of her first relationship. She was persuaded that time away was just what she needed. Kate was thrilled to hear that she was coming out for two months. Kate's account continues:

We had a really good few days prior to Ruth's arrival at Denpassar. I hired a car for when she arrived and we went out to all the places I had been shown when I first came to Bali. She – Ruth – has acclimatized really well to the heat, but still can't quite get her head around 'the creepy crawlies'. She's even scared of the geckos! One guy tried to explain that they and the spiders are her friends as they eat the mozzies – but was she having any of it?

We spent a week in Bali before leaving for Sulawesi, and here we are, Ujung Ladang, having done quite a harsh road trip through the country and returned to our entry point, waiting to get a boat to Flores. We passed through the interior fairly fast, taking in a bit of culture on the way – against the grain? Nah! We stayed in Toraja, an

Live pig offering at Torajan funeral.

area in the mountains of central Sulawesi, and got invited to a funeral, sounds fun, I know, but actually the highlight of their social season! Families spend up to two years from the death of a relative saving to afford the funeral to buy the beasts to slaughter. Ours was a very well to do family and a lot is expected. People come from miles around over the course of a few days with their offerings, buffalo, boar, the pigs carried on stick.

Thankfully we missed the grand slaughter – enough of a sight to see the animals 'waiting'. We took sugar!! It felt very strange to be included in what is to us a very personal mourning. Anyway, with the funeral, and enough traditional villages to tire anyone we left the culture zone, stopping along the way, but with the aim of getting to 'the Togians'– a group of islands in the Tomini Bay separating north and central Salawesi.

Daughter of the deceased dressing for the funeral.

They are so special, the only place in Indonesia, and one of few in the world with Fringe, Atoll and Barrier Reef, so loads of snorkeling and diving and of course very paradisiacal. We stayed in Kadiri, not yet in the *Lonely Planet* but sure to be soon. From the mainland we took a boat (local boat) for 36 hours – Ruth's first experience of being anywhere without other travellers (and really seemed to enjoy it!), sleeping on the deck with all the usual chickens and cargo and other passengers, and their interest in the 'strangers'. It was a really fun trip, and then another boat to get us to Kadidiri, so beautiful – you can't imagine – and I got her snorkeling!

We bought equipment in Bali, the first few times she swam like she was in a race – not looking at a thing and I'd find her back on the shore! Then at the end we (plus five others) got a boat to take us to Taipi – a tiny island with reef all around. I think the fact that there were so many in the water all together helped? But anyway we all snorkeled around the island in an hour or so, and OK she was second back – but she did it. It does take some getting used to and I still have the odd palpitation in sharky waters! The funniest thing was seeing two snakes in one day. The first an eight or nine foot python, but thankfully dead. But then what they call 'an hour snake' as when it bites you're dead in an hour. It fell into the restaurant and we were watching from the beach, some macho guys were chasing it out when it dawned on us they were chasing it our way!

We made some good friends in Togian and I would love to go back but time pressed. Anyway, a lot of travelling and some sore bones later we're back in the south and sad to be leaving, but still to come are Flores, Sumba, maybe Sumbawa, and Lombok.

I don't know if I'll be back for Christmas or not. Can't wait to see the new house – Christian and Francis had moved – and all of you. Hope you can be bothered to read all of this.

We'll be back in Bali on 7th December,

All my love, Kate.

PS We're staying in a really nice hotel – with bath – and I'm drawing my first one since 11 August 1998.

It was now mid December. When she first arrived in Bali in early October, Ruth met friends of Kate's prior to exploring; one was a young

Frenchman, Alain.

On their return to Bali, as Ruth prepared to come home, they all met up again. Kate enjoyed Alain's company, but it was purely platonic. Kate wrote the following in a letter to Lucy, her old friend from David Hicks in England, who subsequently passed it on to us.

Dear Lucy

So much has happened in the last three weeks; things that make anything else seem trivial. It's rather a long story – and also a little upsetting.

Among the group in Bali was this French guy, Alain – nice, but nothing in it on my part, he asked me to meet him in a bar down the road so I said I'd be there in an hour – I don't know why but I changed my mind and didn't go. I left a note on his door – 'sorry, see you tomorrow'. But the next day it was still there – more unusually I didn't see him all day – that night I asked some people at reception and they seemed strange – but I didn't think too much more about it. Still I didn't see him so I went to ask again – Lucy, it was horrible, they told me he was dead. He'd had a motorbike accident that night – I found out later he'd got really drunk in the bar and crashed just around the corner.

This is nearly three weeks ago and I'm feeling a lot better about it now but still it's ongoing. To be very removed I'll just tell you the story – you see he had told me that his passport was bought – so obviously not in his name or anything so I had to go to the French Consul and fill them in – it's all been very above my head and the Consul, I think, has been playing some quite serious games with me – thinking that I'm involved. (I don't know if this is the kind of thing you'll be expecting to hear in a letter from me but it's been the main thing happening here, so it's all my news and I'd completely forgotten I'd promised to send you a letter pre-Stefan arriving.)

Anyway, the Consul quizzed me for all I knew and told me I should leave, not only Bali, but Indonesia – why? – because he thought it was murder. At that point he really made me feel like he was my aide and on my side – kept me away from the police and seemed very straightforward – now I don't know. My mind is so jumbled with everything it all comes out in the wrong order and I forget

Ruth and Kate up Keli Mutu, Flores, 4am!

to include so much – anyway, I did a lot of investigative work – people originally unwilling to help when I was with the Consul – in the bar they hadn't seen him, etc, etc. But I knew he was there because he was waiting for me. So I went later on my own and got a lot more information. Lots of story behind everything but it would take pages. Suffice to say I feel terrible.

The night before he died he had said how much he liked me, and needed me, but I had said I just enjoyed his friendship. There was lots more said and with all that ringing in my head I've really been driven to find out what happened, and sort everything out here for him – it makes me feel better but with a guy like him easier said than done. Firstly, he was on the run from France – so these Consul/Embassy people, while extremely useful to the likes of you and me – can turn out to be extremely manipulative, uncaring, and even callous machines – only out to get what they want. We had the cremation last week and now he won't release the ashes – despite five notifications from Alain's sister in France that that is her wish. It seems they want her to suffer for her brother's misdoings.

It's really crappy Lucy – I was supposed to pack up his room – yet the one time they knew I wouldn't be around was during the cremation – so they packed it all up and are holding that too. It's all so complicated and I'm not explaining very well – sorry – I think it will have to wait till I get home.

Lots of love till then,

Kate

Boat trip to Tai Pai, November 1998.

Stefan arrived in Bali as planned, two days after Kate wrote that letter. Ruth was there for a further week, but was quite freaked out by what had happened and was glad to be flying home for Christmas. She said little to me about this darker side of their adventures. I only heard about the terrible incident with the Frenchman much later. My instinct, when I did, was to think, Gosh Kate, with a shudder. Her trusting nature meant she got swept up in things she didn't need to. There was no such thing as a lost cause in Kate's book.

7

THAILAND

Dear All   January 1999
Here I am now on a small island in Thailand looking out to sea, through the palm trees on to the green turquoise waters of Asia.

It was a last minute decision to come, I suddenly felt the need to leave Indonesia, see something new and stay with friends – so in a mad rush I packed up my past six months (most had to be given away!) and got probably the most expensive ticket from Denpasar to Bangkok – shock!

Bangkok is huge – I mean vast. Luckily Stefan has a friend living here (with a Thai girlfriend) who met us at the airport, no trying to get cheap transport, without knowing what cheap is, in a new country, with a new currency and ripe for the ripping off unfortunately; the Thai girlfriend didn't quite get the backpacker economy thing – with the usual assumption that white meant rich. We spent one night in a great hotel before finding our way to the Kao San Road and all the economy accommodation and all that goes with, that anyone can stand. It's hot and hectic, street food, markets, tut-tuts (motorized rickshaws) and very below standard rooms (Indonesia was such a joy – I couldn't believe how big, clean and good the rooms were) – anyway, Bangkok wore us all pretty thin – there's so much going on. It's an experience and a half really, anything goes.

There's a huge skin trade, floating markets, Singaporean type high-rises, palaces, temples, canals, poverty, everything all in one – and millions of tailors! Then there are all the 'lady boys' etc. We went to a real red light street on our first night with a couple of people, sat in a street bar and hardly said a word to each other, all just sat wide-eyed at the sights. There are beautiful silks and velvets – everything a squillionth of the price at home.

I sent Dad back a birthday present – possibly a bit garish – but very Bangkok – by the way, the script says 'Kimono'! hope it got there. Am sending one, miniature, exactly the same – Charlie size, so Charlie can copy Pompa and Poppy's got some gorgeous little Chinese style pyjamas in pink silk. I'd love to see them in them.

Bangkok didn't even last a week for us. Thailand is very different from Indonesia, it's very touristy and we haven't found any special places yet that haven't been packed out with backpackers.

So, a long bus journey – a few hours on a boat, and on to Ko Tao – a lot more tourism than you might expect but for good reason, it's beautiful, trees, rocks, beaches, boats, very small, lots of fish (not such exciting coral) but a delight after Bangkok.

Having ditched the hammock I made in Indonesia I had to buy another. Swinging on my balcony I've stitched, patched and pinned my way back to a half reasonable wardrobe, three hours this morning washing out a million memories (plus two hours yesterday so I'd have something to wear today).

I was beginning to feel fit and healthy again until edging over some slippery rocks, to go snorkeling, two days ago, my feet going, and smashing my back and elbows on the way down before plunging into the water – I'm now stiff and bruised and have lots to clean and cream every night! Don't worry though – it wasn't bad enough to stop me snorkeling! A friend and I had gone to that area to see sharks; mostly black tipped – reef sharks – I did get a little nervous that the normally disinterested black tips may frenzy at a sniff of my blood, but was reassured (shouldn't listen to a man from landlocked Switzerland on the psychology of sharks?!) by Rowland. Possibly the place would be 'shark island' which is a rock that lies off the south east coast.

My bungalow is sweet, a bedroom and bathroom. I have a house cat – electricity from 6pm-1am, a few elusive mice that chew my wallet, and of all things my soap, and yesterday went for 7am ablutions got back into bed for further snooze, the idea of which halted abruptly at the sight of 'Lola' the look-alike tarantula – big hairy spider the size of my hand, who had somehow managed to infiltrate the calm confines of my mosquito net. How long had she been there? Help was needed and an obliging early rising Thai was called in, even he, before seeing her, and assuring me there were no dangerous spiders on Ko Tao, or in my net, very nervously and behind protection, tensed as he moved in – Lola gone and adrenalin still going –

the snooze urge had gone and I seem now to have got back into my pre-Bangkok early mornings.

There's not much more to tell of Ko Tao as yet but I'm moving again. I'm sure the letters will be more frequent.

All my love to everyone, another Happy Birthday to Dad, Look after yourself (and yourselves everyone),

All my love, Kate.

Dear Ruthie   January 1999?

Well it's 11pm and I'm sitting on a cushion on the floor of my hut. I can hear the sea lapping on the shore and someone is strumming on a guitar nearby. We're on 'Bottle Beach' but I haven't figured out why the name. It's about as remote as I've seen Thailand get – but still not very. The only access is by boat as we're backed on to mountains of thick rainforest (a paradise for snakes and spiders – you'd love it!!) There's no electricity and still they manage to fill about 80 bungalows. Most people come and go in a few days but there are still the long termers. Stefan and I have been here a while and show no signs of leaving. It's very calm, no waves at all – like Togians but nothing to see really so I use the fins ever day to have a high powered swim to the other side of the bay and back (about a mile, impressive?)

On the far side of the bay is 'The Rock' which we climb sometimes and have a view for miles (we're on an island and you can see Koh Samui and Koh Tao miles away). It's a sweaty business and a precarious climb at the top of the rock – but so stunning – you can see practically the whole island behind you.

I've been playing Frisbee daily as well and have got into this annoying habit of getting up at 6.30 every morning.

We went into town two weeks ago and got stranded as the boats weren't working – rough weather. We found two other Bottle Beachers in the same predicament and chartered a 4x4 to get as close as possible on the other side of the hills. Stefan had no shoes and six litres of water in his pack, the sun had gone down and not a torch between us. We walked for two hours using lighters to light the roots and undergrowth and try and see the places where the land fell away and arrived back cut, bruised, hot and tired at 9pm and no snake encounters! (They're building a restaurant and have just caught a four metre black python whose skin they're using as deco above the bar!). On to creepy crawlies now (just for you!) I had a scorpion in my bathroom last week who, in the time it took me to go for help disappeared, giving me a great night's sleep wondering where to? I was woken two nights ago by lots of noises, then something landed on my foot through the net – a heart attack and mad panic finding a torch, revealed a rat – playfully pursued by a large cat. And there was the mammoth spider I found hanging off the balcony – it was Linda's birthday – so I prodded a bit (with tweezers and spoon) and yes he was dead, so on a lovely sand background I superglued eight legs, bulging body and funny pincery things on to a piece of card, popped it into an envelope and presented it to Linda (no joke – it's body was bigger than my thumb and legs like pipe cleaners – tarantula style but brown).

Linda's birthday was great (I think everyone used it as an excuse to do something – and we spent days planning it). There's a guy who organizes chess tournaments – Stefan is completely undefeated in every game – and he organized one of the fishing trawlers to come and take sixteen of us out for the day – snorkeling, swimming and fishing (rod, not trawling!). I caught a shell but believe it or not it's actually good fun. There were acrobatic diving competitions off the roof and we grilled each catch as it came on board. In the evening we had a surprise party for her – a huge barbecued fish, fireworks and bonfire.

I've set up an email number (curlykate68@hotmail.com) but have only used it once as we're staying in a place accessible only by boat with no electricity so no telephones or computers. Anyway, we ventured out two days ago – more in a minute – and I had a go then. I pay per minute to try and find how the b***** things work – and left when the price got too high without having done much at all.

The reason we'd ventured out is that the movie *The Beach* is being made in Thailand by the same director from *Trainspotting* and starring Leonardo DiCaprio (shame not Matt Dillon or anyone else really!) You remember that book about an English guy who gets given a hand-drawn map leading him to a secret little beach in Thailand –

Sunset at Labuan Bajo, Flores.

dark side of paradise type stuff?

They were looking for extras and a few speaking parts – 'traveller looks, just be yourselves'. You should have seen it – people doing voice exercises on the beach outside, girls tarted up to the nines with full make up – the exact opposite of the 'traveller look'. They asked for contact numbers! And got a lot of email addresses – Stefan put Bottle Beach. They could have said 'don't call us we'll call you' but said 'check your email in 7-10 days' – so if I can be bothered to get the boat to the village where I can get a lift to the town where I can use a computer, and after all that succeed – then I could be on the big screen within a few weeks, doing goodness knows what – whatever it is that 'traveller look' people do!*

Stefan is running very low on money so will have to head back to Switzerland, and I don't feel inspired to explore Thailand further. I shall probably head back to Indonesia or home.

With Christian's birthday looming I've spent a couple of days making her a card from what little I can find here – but it looks really

---

* Kate made it as 'girl in a phone box' but it passed in a flash. When home, she and Ruth went to see the film but failed to identify Kate.

good – I think! It's a collage of all natural things, sand, palm leaves, coconut matting – of our house and the scenery – like being in kindergarten again! Goodness knows if I'll get it to her for the 30th.

This is turning into another of my epic letters, so I'll sign off and I may see you before this does. Hope you're all well, love to you all,

All love, Kate.

Kate returned home in April 1999 and got straight to work. Amazingly, despite her frequent absences, she was still being asked to do design jobs by various clients in London and in between re-decorated our spare rooms and generally lent a helping hand. Once again she spent as much time as she could with Christian, Francis, Poppy and Charlie, catching up with friends and walking the dogs over the fells.

A major decision was made to buy herself a camper van that she could call home wherever she might be in Britain or 'mainland Europe'. Kate used that expression twenty odd years ago and I remember thinking how foreign it sounded at the time.

After much research, helped by the Caravan Club, which she joined, and the AA, she went to Liverpool to pick up the chosen vehicle – a Hymer. She was incredibly excited about it, which was quite infectious, and we all lent ourselves to discussion as to how best to give it a 'makeover'. In fact, Kate had such a strong instinct, that she actually tackled everything single-handed. With the carpentry skills she had acquired as an apprentice joiner and the manual she bought to teach herself about plumbing, she completely stripped out the interior and put in shower, loo, carpets, cushions, Indian sheets, bedding, pot plants. For birthday presents she was given colour-coordinated towels, kitchen equipment, etc., which of course she chose.

Everything had its place and was as tidy as any ship. She carried backgammon, chess, scrabble, packs of cards, books galore and masses of maps and snowboard and snorkeling gear. She re-wired, putting in a sound system and television. Just inside the 'front' door she fixed a slate where she assiduously wrote jobs to be done. It was equipped to cover any contingency and she was justifiably proud of it – it took her months to get it to the exacting standard she set herself.

On the dashboard, completely resurfaced, was the place for the inevitable mug of tea, ciggies and tapes within easy reach of the driver's seat.

One of the many bonuses of her 'home from home' was that she and Ruth could go to local weddings, park up the camper with the other guests' cars and continue to party all night, after everything had closed down. They gave a few private parties with the camper in this fashion during 1999 and 2000.

Kate had even made the Hymer cosy enough to withstand winter temperatures in the Alps. In December Kate was on her way through Europe in her camper van – on her way to visit Stefan – and made an arrangement with Ruth to divert to Chambery, not much off her route to Switzerland, to join a party of their friends who were skiing in Courchevel.

She arrived in the dark, in a blizzard, and the van came to an abrupt halt in the middle of the town. The only thing to do was to lock it up and find her sister. After a real jolly, five of them went back to the camper van to continue the merriment and spend the night there.

The following morning there was a knock on the door and a policeman requested Kate move the vehicle as it was parked on a roundabout – which of course had been indistinguishable in thick snow in the dark the previous evening. Kate replied that they would have to tow them off or leave them as the battery was dead.

Two of the party went to find Ruth's hire car to jump-start the camper but couldn't locate it because they were all buried in snow. Eventually they went to the police station where they were told it had been impounded because it was illegally parked. They were in luck because it was a special day in France so they need not pay the fine! However, it was in a compound a mile away.

Ruth's mini break was not enhanced when Kate – who couldn't ski because of a dodgy cruciate ligament in her knee but snow boarded – requested that Ruth use her ski stick to tow her along the flat, of which there was rather a lot. Ruth is a reasonably experienced skier and was itching to spend every possible minute on the slopes.

Very sadly Kate and Stefan were reaching something of an

impasse. She was feeling ready to settle down, but he, while wanting to stay with her, did not show the same inclination.

They were soul mates, but there were one or two fundamental differences. This meant that they were often a good foil for one another, but it also led to stand-offs. Stefan was very un-worldly. Kate had strong opinions about life, the universe and the state of the nation, which she liked to discuss. Stefan was not interested in politics or the economy; he had a gentle, hippy-ish attitude to life. He was a wanderer, who at the time just wanted to keep on exploring.

Stefan was totally non-confrontational; in time of war he would probably be a conscientious objector. He would definitely walk away from trouble. Kate on the other hand would take things head on; if she perceived any injustice she would stand up and be counted. Stefan said she would sometimes try to fix things with a sledgehammer. He, in turn, infuriated her with his apathy. Both hugely creative, unconventional, eccentric, and certainly free spirits, they were very good together. They had some blazing rows during this time, which would simply blow over.

She felt she did not want to spend the rest of her life on a motorbike and in a tent. Much as she liked backpacking and living frugally on a few dollars a day, she didn't want to spend her whole life leading a nomadic existence. Kate gave Stefan an ultimatum, but after the initial brickbats they remained very close. As a consequence their relationship drifted apart. The timing was wrong.

Kate was devastated, although few knew how deeply. I think she would have liked to marry Stefan and start a family. But it was not to be.

8

BACK TO BALI

We spent a family Christmas and New Year, seeing in 2001 at Black Dub. After much thought, Kate had decided she would move to Bali, making it her second home. Several things had influenced this decision, some of which are conjecture based on the Kate we know, and some are based on letters we have seen since her disappearance.

She loved Stefan deeply, and although she was so forthright in her views and opinions, she was equally a very sensitive person whose feelings were easily hurt. She wanted to settle down and he didn't; the age-old impasse. Stefan later said Kate had turned his life around from a negative to a positive. She had been instrumental in helping him come to terms with difficulties in his life and brought him back from a 'dark place'.

Being so responsive to sadness, vibrations, atmosphere and climatic changes could be too much, leading to fears and worries. At these times, Kate needed to withdraw into a world of tranquillity and peace; she did seek to live an elusive and ideal lifestyle.

Western politics depressed her. She had grown up with wars raging in the Falklands, Bosnia, The Gulf, Iraq. Margaret Thatcher had been in power for most of Kate's life and her acquisitive, 'me first' society as she saw it, just left her cold. Her personal style offended Kate, although both felt passionately about traditional family values. But Mrs Thatcher's attitude was too Victorian and austere, for Kate, who thought the she was domineering, inflexible and abrasive.

With the emphasis on materialism, defence, privatization and VAT, and the battle with the unions and appalling urban riots, Kate saw Mrs Thatcher as a dictator, whereas she herself was an idealist. She would not allow that the Prime Minister did much for Britain, putting the economy back on its feet and making home ownership possible for many. Mrs Thatcher had strength of conviction and made us a stronger and more confident nation, but there were casualties, massive unemployment being one.

Kate and I talked for hours about this during our late night chats. She thought politicians were deluded liars, who at best served their own interests. If there was a dark side to Kate, it was a horror of what human beings were capable of doing to each other. She struggled to comprehend, let alone deal with it.

The more disenchanted she became, the more drawn she was towards a utopia; political ideals promoting universal equality, global co-operation, the world operating in unison. This was a vision increasingly at odds with the daily atrocities one heard of on the news: famine in Somalia, the war in Sierra Leone, the rumours about al Qaeda.

Kate's view of the world had fundamentally changed as a result of all her travelling. It was more than disillusionment about our greedy capitalist society or disenchantment with western values. Western standards seemed artificial, vacuous. She didn't feel she fitted in any more.

Of course I tried to change her mind; did my best to persuade her to stay, to look again at what was good in England. I knew it wasn't a personal rejection, she was still as attached to home and family as ever. But I had been aware for some time how uncomfortable she was at the local drinks parties or get-togethers in Cumbria. She was restless, a butterfly. I listened to her reasoning and in the end I had to let her go.

Bali appeared to be the place where she would find the tranquility she craved, with time to sort out her emotions and thoughts on life. It had beaches and mountains, nightlife and solitude, all within one tiny island. She loved the warmth of the sun, the vibrant colour, the gamelan music, the traditional dance, the spicy food – being there made her feel alive. Buddhism had long been a draw; she was enchanted by the offerings to the spirits outside every shop or café. She loved the gentleness of the Balinese and historically and ethnologically it was clear that it suited her.

Finally, following years of discomfort, she had addressed the knee

*Above, Eilean Donan, Kyle of Lochalsh and below,
Skye from Eilean.*

problem which had plagued her. After being admitted to the Accident and Emergency ward in chronic pain, her cruciate ligament had been operated on by an eminent surgeon at the Chelsea and Westminster hospital. It remained vulnerable and she carried knee supports, but it gave her a real boost of confidence.

She packed up her camper van and went on a 'road trip', saying goodbye to friends all over England and Scotland. She took photographs of things typically English; signposts around home and the Lake District where she spent so much time; phone boxes, post boxes, the dogs, cows in fields, the family house near Keswick. She gathered the family in the drawing room, got Gran out of her residential home, set the timer on her very superior camera, and took a portrait photograph of us all together.

Kate had persuaded us to buy a computer and she set it up while at Black Dub. I reluctantly agreed to an introductory session on this new thing called 'email'. She had assured me that sending hand-written airmail letters to far-flung Poste Restantes would be a thing of the past; this would be how we'd stay in touch. I found it a complete nightmare at first; my typing was – and still is – slow. But she was absolutely right and with perseverance I progressed.

Early in 2001, Kate left for Indonesia with a large amount of money in her bank account in England, having scrimped and saved for months. She stocked up with underwear at Marks and Spencer, packed up a fully comprehensive medical kit, and most importantly, her life story in seven large fully annotated photo albums. She took two enormous rucksacks. We said goodbye with heavy hearts.

She planned to live temporarily in Kuta, the mecca for Australian tourists, while looking for somewhere to rent. Then there was the small business of working out what shape her life should take. Given that the Indonesian economy was almost bankrupt, she did not foresee a financial problem. Apart from what she'd saved from her design work, the girls were also gifted generous sums each year by their grandmother.

Tobi, Lucy's brother, had been persuaded by Kate to accompany her out there. It would give him the chance to see the country and give her some help with the move. Tobi had never been to Bali before and this was his chance with a real old hand who proved her credentials from the word go. At Denpassar, Bali's main airport, there seemed to be a problem with Kate's passport, but Kate was having none of it. She asked in fluent Balinese if she could speak to the guard's superior.

When she finally got the chief in front of her, she explained that she was not prepared to pay the bribe (200 cigarettes) which the man was asking for and demanded her right as a British national with all the correct paperwork to get her and her friend's passport stamped. Miraculously the 'problem' just disappeared. Similarly she did not accept the taxi driver who tried the 'meter not working' trick. Kate just explained politely in Balinese, that she had been to the country on several previous occasions and knew what to do; she lent over, pressed a few buttons on the meter and miraculously it was fixed.

In Kuta they stayed in Kate's favourite budget 'chalet' complex – a dozen or so small, but clean, whitewashed bungalows in a little garden. Each had a double and single bed and a hole-in-the-floor loo which doubled as a shower. The complex was walled with a small open-air bar and simple restaurant. It made an ideal base. Most days were spent exploring, introducing Tobi to some of her old friends, with the evening starting at the Sari Bar (the one which was later blown up by extremists). From this mostly European bar they would explore a little deeper into the maze of alleyways known as gangs, before winding up in one of the many Balinese nightclubs to dance and chat.

Kate had a sensible regime in the mornings that she insisted they stuck to. They tidied their belongings away, swept the room and then sprayed ant repellent into every nook, crevice, windowsill and doorway. Having got Tobi acclimatized to Balinese life, she suggested they hire a car and go to see some of the other parts of the island. They hired a 'real bone-shaker of a jeep' and set off for Ubud, the cultural capital. Kate had a mantra when packing for these sorts of trips – 'take only the things you really need', so they left the majority of their belongings in the room in Kuta which they'd decided to keep as a base. Having had their fill of temples and monkeys, they moved on to Padangbai to watch the longtail boats and persuade the fishermen to sell them their catch.

Back in Kuta, Kate introduced Tobi to Eduard, who owned 'Hot Chillie', a very smart internet café, which she regularly frequented. He had a day off so suggested they go to 'Dreamlands' a beautiful beach, largely untouched (at the time) by the property developers of Kuta. When they went to turn off the main road on to a tiny dusty track they found it blocked by a makeshift barrier, behind which stood two very small 'policemen'. They demanded money to be let through.

After a quick exchange in Balinese, Eduard and Kate sat, their arms folded. 'They're not real policeman,' Kate said. 'They get their mothers to make uniforms and then they're sent out to fine/extort money from unsuspecting tourists.' Apparently they made them wait for about ten minutes, then raised the barrier and laughed. Kate said Stefan had once got a fine for having his motorbike light on during the day. There was endless petty corruption on Bali and Kate had seen it all. There were 'no flies on Kate – they wouldn't dare', as Tobi said to me in a letter which I received later.

That week they met Richard Behar, who was to become a good friend. He invited them up to the Holiday Inn where he was staying. It was his last night there before moving down to their complex which he liked much more. Little could they have known on this night, when they celebrated their friendship, that Richard would later have to use all his world-wide contacts as an investigative journalist for *Fortune* magazine New York, to help Cumbrian police with their investigation into Kate's disappearance. He was a senior writer, specialising in investigations for *Fortune* magazine.

Richard had written a few investigative stories from Jakarta. His government contacts in Jakarta were a little dusty, but numbered US government sources, FBI agents and various security experts. He hoped one or any of them might be able to suggest something to help. Richard was much in touch with our police initially, but in spite of doing everything he could it was of no avail. Tobi who is an extremely talented professional photographer would also play a hugely

Travelling by dug out between islands.

significant role taking photographs at the memorial service to celebrate her life. But for now they were just young people having fun
without a care in the world. They spent that evening together and indulged, with Richard's blessing, on his *Fortune* expenses account.

Tobi returned home and Kate set about making a permanent home
on the island. It meant a lot that he later wrote a long letter to me
about their adventures together. I was delighted to hear of Kate's flu-
ency in the language and confidence with the Balinese people. Out-
wardly strong, even 'Amazonian', inwardly sensitive and anxious to
love and be loved, this independent young western woman was extremely vulnerable; for someone well-travelled she was actually child-
like, a naivety that could so easily get her into trouble.

In June 2001 Kate rang to say she had news; she was engaged. To whom? What nationality? What did he do? There was, of course, a torrent of questions. He was called Joseph, he was Peruvian, and he was a professional surfer. His parents had a coffee plantation in Peru; he owned a hotel in Peru but a manager was running it; his father was an architect, his brother a lawyer. I think he had another brother and a sister.

Kate made him speak to us on the phone. He said little and it meant nothing; he might have been shy and being bounced into talking to us must have been a little nerve-wracking. Kate was excited and desperately wanted us to meet him. She was coming home in August and hoped he would come too.

I didn't know what to say. I felt instantly worried but tried not to let it show in my voice. Peruvian or Balinese – it wouldn't really have made much difference, it was a culture we didn't know. She was intending to marry a man she had met thousands of miles away, but it could have been a million miles away. It seemed so remote, but Kate was so persuasive over the phone and we just wanted her to be happy. They were designing an engagement ring. The plan was that they would rent a house and both of them find jobs.

In the weeks to come, Kate found a charming little house outside Kuta, but not too remote. It was in Uluwatu, Jimbaran, not far from the sea. On the property was another smaller house where the maid, Ketut, and her family lived. As was customary a maid came with the rented accommodation to look after the property. Kate loved it and set about making it her home. With her flair for textiles and some imagination it was soon lovely.

She sent us a collection of photographs taken from every conceivable angle. It was reassuring to see where she was living. It made it seem more real. The house was approached by a lengthy track through a small settlement of traditional Balinese houses and one or two more modern bungalows. Right at the end, slightly removed, was the house that Kate had found – an attractive property.

It was walled and entry was through a stone doorway. Her house was on the right, traditional, quite western, almost colonial. In front of it was a small courtyard and opposite, on the left, was the maid's house. To one corner of the house was a small wing containing a single storey bedroom and washroom, and on the far side of the courtyard at right angles to her house was a shrine, with a Buddha, elevated on a few steps and standing about six feet high. The photographs showed a warm welcoming house, cosy, with cornicing around the ceilings, panelled doors and grey stone tiled floors. I could entirely see why it had appealed to her.

Kate furnished it combining traditional Bali 'antique' furniture with wonderful textiles; soft woven throws and beautiful intricately embroidered wall hangings. On every sofa and chair there were vibrant-coloured cushions in orange, ocean and sky blues, and yellows. The spacious sitting room was separated from the kitchen by a bar, floor to table height, on which stood a glass-fronted cupboard, storing interesting artefacts and earthy-coloured ceramic bowls.

Her bedroom and bathroom were on the ground floor, the former having traditional Balinese carved bookcases, and again vibrant throws – lovely against fresh white cotton sheets and pillowcases. At the top of the staircase, leading off the sitting room, was a covered balcony from which you see what looked like jungle; lush trees and ferns, quite dense around the back and one side of the house, but sufficiently removed to allow the sun to bathe the property. Just off this balcony was a third large bedroom with four-poster bed and shower room. Much to Kate's delight, Ketut, the maid had two young children.

Kate was paying for it all, and installed a computer and phone line in the belief that Joseph would get a job and eventually contribute. She herself had thoughts about working from home and was exploring possibilities. Of particular interest was the idea of exporting Balinese furniture back to the UK, where she could see there was a ready market. With her eye for design and excellent contacts in the interiors business it could have been the making of her.

We would talk about it when she came home in August.

9

WEDDING PLANS

In August 2001 Kate came home without Joseph. He had got around to telling her that he was in the process of divorcing his wife, who lived in Lima with their seven-year old son George. His brother, a lawyer, was overseeing the case. But Joseph had no money, owed his wife maintenance, wanted to see his son, plus he had 'business' to attend to in Peru. Kate thought it was very laudable that he wanted the contact with his child and encouraged him to go back. She lent him £5,000 to fly there, while she was in Britain making wedding plans. It was to cover his debts, including what he owed his wife.

Kate arrived home in great spirits and seemed very happy entering into all the family activities, seeing her niece and nephew, watching Ruth eventing and visiting friends in her camper van. She was forever out in the yard, working on her beloved Hymer, fine-tuning it and making adjustments here and there.

We discussed the wedding. Early on I had tentatively asked if she was imagining something exotic on a beach in Bali, but was quickly put right. There was no doubt in her mind that it should be in Cumbria in the home she knew and loved. In so many ways she was very traditional.

She wanted a Humanist ceremony up on the fell, then afterwards back to Black Dub for the party. She showed me the design for the engagement ring which they were going to commission from a jeweller on Bali. We looked at endless pictures of wedding dresses – page after page of exquisite, beaded, delicate dresses, again surprisingly traditional. It was one of those moments you dream of as a mother and I did my best to put my worries on hold and just enjoy the moment.

She rang Joseph at intervals and could not raise him. At first it didn't concern her – she had always said trust was fundamental to a good relationship – and he had a lot to sort out in Peru. As time went on, she became more and more worried. Eventually, in a state of great agitation she managed to find a telephone number for his family, goodness knows how, but she was tenacious. She rang his mother in Lima, assuming, since he had told her he had given them all the news on Kate and their plan to get married, that she would at least know to whom she was talking. Not at all; not only had she never heard of Kate, she said he already had a wife, and there was certainly no talk of divorce. Her attitude softened as Kate sensitively worked her way round to talking about Joseph.

She was an educated woman – I forget whether they conversed in Spanish or English – but slowly Kate persuaded Joseph's mother to open up to her. We later learned that his family history, as he told it, was all true. His father had owned a coffee plantation, but had moved into the city where he worked as an architect. They had moved to Lima from the countryside because of kidnap threats to his family – not unusual in that part of the world.

The major untruth was his own history, becoming apparent as it unfolded to Kate through his mother. He was the black sheep of the family, had problems with drugs and caused great distress. He was qualified as a chef and they were grateful for that. As the two women who loved him talked, they reassured each other that there was good in him.

On his return to Peru, the wretched man, armed with Kate's money must have got into a lot of trouble, probably both carrying and taking drugs. His family had him taken into a rehabilitation clinic in Peru; no one knew of Kate's existence so they had not informed her. She had no way of knowing where he was or what he was doing, until she got hold of his mother. If she had not had the temerity to track down his family she would have been in the dark for a great deal longer. Kate loved deeply and with great loyalty, however misguided. She was not about to give up on Joseph. There were a lot of tears, a lot of slammed doors. It was hard to console her, because she didn't want consolation.

After she'd shut herself away in her room for a day or two we started to talk again. It was clear that she had no idea about this other life of his. She was very angry he had not been straight with her about his marital situation, let alone a drug problem that he had forgotten to mention. She said they occasionally smoked some marijuana together but nothing more. He had never taken any cocaine in front of her and she was baffled that she hadn't seen the warning signs.

We talked a lot about it; obviously we were extremely concerned. Kate admitted that he had lied to her compulsively, but felt that could be explained by his addiction to cocaine which she had known nothing about, but for which he was now seeking help. She was convinced his love for her was genuine and she could help him; they would get through this.

He was clean, not on drugs, when Kate met him and the relationship had been happy until she came home to discuss the wedding plans. Then he appears to have gone AWOL. Apparently the night before she left he had seemed very wound-up, aggressive, not his usual self at all, which she had naively put down to their impending separation.

I've since seen his letters from these early months and I have to admit that during their whirlwind courtship he appears to have been in love with her. Certainly there was an intimacy and fondness in his tone. There was no hint at that early stage of the monster in him that would manifest itself, the dark side to his character that his family had long known about.

Kate returned to Bali at the beginning of November 2001. All marriage plans had been put on hold while Joseph continued his rehabilitation back in Peru. Kate was in a sort of limbo, but in the meantime she had a home on the island and needed to follow up some work leads she had been pursuing. Having been surrounded by dogs as she was growing up, Kate was determined to find herself a pet, even though most Indonesians considered them vermin. On her return she was invited to see a litter of Weimaraner puppies that had been bred by an American family. Of course she couldn't resist and went home with a bitch puppy which she called Maizie.

Her daily routine, as it developed, was quite fastidious. She was usually up early for her boiled eggs and coffee. Food was important to her and was purchased locally every day. She had had an absolute aversion to supermarket shopping ever since I could remember and took great pleasure in buying fresh produce from local shops or small-holders who were in abundance in Indonesia. Bananas, coconuts, peanuts and black rice could easily be purchased, often straight from the people who grew them.

Since the start of her travels she'd become increasingly frugal, with a deep aversion to what she referred to as 'rip-off Britain'. In Cumbria, she was a nightmare to take to town for general shopping for her own requirements. It didn't improve when I was offering to pay for something; she couldn't bear to spend my money either, so we invariably came back empty-handed and exhausted.

Communication with her extensive network of friends was a most important part of her daily life on Bali. She made frequent visits to her Dutch friend, Eduard, at the Hot Chilli Internet Café, e-mailing friends around the world, many of whom stayed with her in Uluwatu. Visitors have always been a big feature in life at Black Dub and it was no different for Kate in her home from home.

Walking was a passion and she spent hours exercising Maizie on the beaches or in the mountains which she loved. Before Maizie's arrival Kate had been as happy walking on her own, with something of the loner in her. I can identify strongly with this as my parents were abroad in my teens. I was at school in the UK and my grandmother, who lived in the Lake District, was my guardian. I spent many happy hours walking the fells with my own thoughts uninterrupted. Much as I knew where Kate's desire to ramble freely came from I was glad to think of her with her dog at her side. Apparently Maizie had recently discovered the joys of swimming both in the sea and in the many freshwater ponds on the island. As a result she was really 'cool in the water – I can take her anywhere'. For Kate too, there was swimming – she was a very powerful swimmer, and regularly drove out to one or other of the less touristy beaches and would swim or snorkel off the reefs for hours. Photography, too, remained a passion.

Dinner, lunch or clubbing with friends, was always on the cards and beach parties were a big part of what went on. She kept her distance from what she saw as the 'ex-pat' scene, a group of people she described as 'escaping from something, just like me'. Although she saw elements of herself in them and liked some of them as individuals, she didn't seek their company en-masse. She liked to pick her friends from outside the herd, from a diverse range of nationalities and viewpoints. Slowly she developed a circle of friends among the semi-permanent residents on the island. All this, while looking for jobs or trying to work out what she could do from home, kept her well occupied.

Dear Gran   12 December 2001

I'm hoping that if I get this off to you today it will arrive in time for Christmas. Amazingly I received a parcel from mum on Saturday, most stuff never arrives if it looks like it contains 'goodies' worth pinching.

The rain has been torrential most of the night. The rainy seasons vary a lot, last year there was barely any – this year – wow! It makes it very humid when it's 'waiting' to rain, and very fresh afterwards. Bali is so lush, very green, very tropical. I seem to have a permanent layer of grease on my face – which, at least, I guess, will keep me young looking.

I guess you heard that I bought a Weimaraner puppy – Maizie? There is also a 'house dog' – Helley. I can hear them both playing madly outside now. It's like *Lady and the Tramp*. Maizie is very beautiful – her class shows. She's grey (almost silver) with very long legs and prances like a horse. Helley is a typical Bali mutt. He has hair like a lamb, is butch and independent and a real street dog.

I think mum has got all inspired by the post actually getting here – and the 'Black Dub Women' are making up a 'Red Cross' Christmas food parcel – I can't wait!

Christian, Francis, Poppy and Charlie were living at Black Dub, hence the collective noun. We put together Marmite, Colman's English mustard powder, Paxo sage and onion stuffing and packets of bread sauce, plus other bits and pieces including treats for Maizie, a dog whistle and hair ties for Kate.

I now have some plans of who to spend Christmas with – but there are two houses (mine and a friends) both wanting to cook, both from different countries, so different ideas about a 'traditional' Christmas lunch. (I did check to see if there were any seats available to England – but decision made as they are all fully booked for weeks). I have been living with no oven – cooking on two gas hobs – most people do here – and my imagination has become stunted as to alternatives of what to eat. Mum and dad have come to the rescue and are giving me the money for Christmas to buy a cooker. YES! So I'm getting a turkey – and blow the Spaniards and their paella, or pasta, or whatever it is they have on the day.

Well, I've finished my coffee (my morning routine, two teas, two eggs, one coffee!), and I have figured I won't be sending this today…

So it is the next morning, Wednesday. The rains didn't last long yesterday, thank goodness. I spent a horrible morning in town doing 'have tos' and a lovely afternoon at a friend's house swimming and larking around. He has some ponds there which Maizie jumped into at first sight – had her first bad experience with an aggressive monkey, and first fun experience with a load of ducks – you can imagine.

Mum was at a drinks party recently and met some Cumbrians whose son is also living here. I'm meeting him today – it turns out a lot of people I know, know him too. Apparently he set up and is running *Surf Time Magazine*. Anyway, it will be lovely to see someone from home. One of his first questions was 'what are you doing for Christmas?' so there might be more backing for the turkey vs paella.

This may not get to you for Christmas so I'm glad I sent the card separately and this should make it for the New Year.

Ketut the maid has recently started to do her job very well – not sure why. Her discovery this morning has been that Helley has been poohing in the temple – NOT good. A bit like a human poohing in the font. Dogs are the lowest of the low here. It is believed that only the lowest forms get carnated to dogs – and that most have miserable lives and suffering. Ooops.

Happy Christmas Gran.

It's 12.15 (midday) here, so it is even Christmas there – I think it is 4am with you. I'm having a relaxing day, not having got home until 3am. I had a turkey dinner at about 1am (!) I wasn't feeling very Christmassy but made myself go to a party at a friend's house. Turned out to be a really good night so I'm glad I made the effort.

I spent Christmas afternoon on the beach and stayed on for the French friend's BBQ. Lobster, snapper, langoustine, octopus – all as fresh as fresh. Delicious. The island is so small and the seafood is abundant and so cheap. All the things that are expensive in England are some of the cheapest here, lovely rices, seafood, amazing spices. It's only the imported stuff that hurts – unfortunately wine, cheese and red meat – oh well!

Joseph never made it back from Peru as he has had a few problems there – but I'm hoping to see him in March – not sure.

Mum and dad told me you have given all of us grandchildren another cheque. Thank you Gran, you've no idea how much it helps us all. I was thinking; I know you like to know that we have all spent it on 'something' (rather than being swallowed into the general living) – well, I could ill-afford Maizie when I got her (and she was flipping expensive) so could we count her as part of what I used the money for? She has been the best 'thing' I got in years and is amazing company as Joseph is away so much.

I want to do bed and breakfast at the house, and put up posters a few days ago but now think they're all wrong. I'm off to town to change them, do my immigration and see a man about some work.

Merry Christmas, Happy New Year, and thank you Gran. I think I'll be back in June for Lucy's wedding and to have my knee 'done'.

All love 'till then,

Kate

Kate's cruciate ligament in the other knee had gone, and she hoped to have the same surgeon operate on it at the Chelsea and Westminster when she came home. All the time Kate was corresponding with Joseph, still in rehab in Peru. She had kept all the letters, which I now have, and am able to quote from directly.

Dear Joseph   13 December 2001
Another day, another letter... Mario came over yesterday morning and took some photos for me (for you actually!) but I want to get some more (+ outside) shots before I send this.

How are you? I spoke to Poca – he said you will be eating a lot and getting loads of exercise. I hope he is right. I had imagined you cooped up almost in a cell. (This is the first mention of the Diaz brothers, two Peruvian friends of Joseph, whose names would ultimately become inextricably linked to her disappearance)

I can't quite get my head around you being there for so long – and I am not sure if it is a good idea for me to come? I would be spending even more money on a relationship that may not even go anywhere. I just can't imagine that I will not see you until May. Perhaps the not being able to see anyone is just in the initial treatment and you may even be allowed out on home visits later?

By the end it will be 7 months that we have been apart. You may not even want to be with me anymore. I can't imagine that my thoughts will change though. In the end it's a good long time to really decide whether we want to spend the rest of our lives together or not.

We haven't had the smoothest of relationships recently – will that have changed with all your treatment? I hope so. In the end (I don't know whether I'm kidding myself) I hope that all the bad things were a result of your stress? I know you've been unhappy about not being able to provide for George, or a life with me... and also for past regrets. I think what you've been doing is escaping from reality through cocaine – another form of 'borradoring' – I don't know.

My head says move on, make another life for myself. This 'borradoring' kills me. Whatever problems you have, have to be faced. There are responsibilities and there is no situation you are in that cannot be worked out. Instead of disappearing and making things worse – why don't you face things? Use the people who are around you instead of running away from them. Things will never get better if you carry on as you have been.

I hope you see your father and that you stick at it until you have resolved some of your differences. If the clinic you are in is not free then I am sure he is footing the bill. You may not have had the best of relationships and there is a lot of forgiving to be done by both parties – but he does love you, you are his son, and he may not be able to tell you but the fact that he cares enough to get you to a clinic says a lot. He probably hasn't known what to do these last few years – a bit like you I guess! And has dealt with things in a less than successful way (again, like you), but none of us are perfect…

My reactions are sometimes confrontational and in a way lead to just as many problems as you're hiding. I find it hard to ask for help, or accept it when it is offered. I put up walls of defence and strike back sometimes when people hurt me. Something I am going to work on over the next few months.

I am going on a self realization(!) mission, I have goals to stop smoking, reduce my wine consumption (damn) and take a look at my life and the things that need some work. Mum sent over a new knee brace so I can get some more exercise. A new gym has opened up so I'm going to force myself to go. Should be easier when I can't sit still for five minutes when I stop smoking. You will see the smoke coming off the machines in Kuta!

Maizie is great. She has meant I can't up and off so easily (Europe is a no go with quarantine) but I think I will leave her here with Ketut if I visit you in Peru where quarantine isn't required. I just think it's too much for her, that journey for a short time.

I have mixed thoughts about what you should do afterwards. I think for George and your family you should stay in Peru – but then cocaine is so readily available and all of your friends seem to be doing the same. It would not be easy to avoid, will you have the will power to say no and avoid it if you stay there. Maybe your family could get you some work there though and so start back on a normal life.

Bali is much harder to get work that pays reasonably but you do not have the option to get cocaine here so easily. But I am here and I would help you stay away from trouble.

Joseph, how did you get into this state? I'm angry with you for getting into this position in the first place. I think what has happened is that you have taken a lot of cocaine, got depressed, got paranoid and lost your way (I have seen you on it remember, the night before you left – and that was only one night…) You were very aggressive and hostile for that last 24 hours. Goodness knows what a few days of taking A LOT would do to you.

There are no problems here for you anymore – everything has been sorted out. Poca told me – I don't know what that all means but probably good for you to know.

I have cut off any contact with your friends over here except for Poca occasionally. There always seems to be bad news with them and they don't make for a peaceful life. Our cultures are so different and I can't stand all the shouting and stress and lying. All of the Latino boys are a mess. If you do come back then I want you to keep all of them at a distance. They all seem to be fighting amongst themselves – and I've seen the way they treat each other (and you).

In a letter from your brother, he said your mother said you are ok – and that you had said it was 'for the best'. He also said you feel 'safer'. I'm not sure why, is that because you are away from drugs? Or is it because you were in some sort of trouble? Or because you don't have to look after yourself any more – no responsibility?

After thinking about it I've decided I won't come over to see you. Better to use this time to get used to you not being here in case you don't come back.

I've decided to pay the rent again, and am getting the car for 1 million a month now – YES! – but never bought the oven and I've taken out the phone line and computer. I'll see how things go and look at things later if we decide to stay together.

Hello Baby   Friday, 21 Deecember 2001
You are doing the right thing. It is time to change the way you live. You are doing now what will affect the way your life will run. No more running. You said you feel much better now and think two months is enough – but we are talking life changes here. There are many years of patterns and habits that go way deeper than a 'quick' fix of two months. Follow the programme through.

I am so proud of you, imagine how your life can be. You'll be able to look in the mirror and like what you see. I know you adore George, and I know you are the best father when you are with him, but the contact and reliability have been lacking – that will never happen again, I'm sure. Do not give up on this time. I am sure there will be points when it is very hard – but look to the light at the end of the tunnel (it will be hard for me too).

You have to live by what you know is good and right, you have to have morals – there are no grades of good and bad. If good and bad were black and white then we will find all the grey we can to justify leaving the path. But morals are how you define yourself.

I still think it would be better if we do our individual journeys for a while. I will call on Christmas Day and your birthday. You must try not to think of me too much and concentrate on where you are and what you are doing.

I am still waiting for the photographs from Raoul and Poca – I know it's sneaky but once I have them I hope never to have anything more to do with them. Low Lifes!!

I see Rodrigo sometimes. He's different from the other Latinos. He's very positive. I have never seen him aggressive – is always forgiving – despite the appalling way others treat him sometimes. (Rodrigo, the only 'nice' Latino in Kate's view, would soon be on the other side of the law too. An easy target, he would later do time in Kerobokan Prison on Bali, for dealing in small amounts of ecstasy.)

You understand that my family is really important to me. They want the best for me – as yours does you. Because they are your family they are really important to me too. I want to have a good relationship with them. I hope I didn't push them too far, I was just so desperate to find you. I hope they understand that.

Lucia, Joseph's brother kept in touch with Kate whilst Joseph was in rehab in Peru. He obviously felt obliged to do something, not least because the family were trying to keep Joseph's most recent fall from grace from their father who was ailing. Although Lucia's contact was minimal and relatively formal, at least it provided her with a link to what was going on. The Victoria Centre, Joseph's rehabilitation unit, was run by a religious order; they shaved his head as part of the cleansing process. Much as Kate supported his stay in the centre at first, over the ensuing weeks she became concerned that it was something of a cult, that he was being brainwashed into turning to God.

Meanwhile she used Lucia as a conduit to get letters to Joseph, as she had been told that she could have no direct contact whilst he was undergoing his treatment.

Dear Lucia   (no date)

Enclosed are a few things for Joseph. I am very grateful for you getting them to him for me. I have left everything open as I am sure the clinic will want to 'inspect' the contents.

Could we still arrange for me to speak to him on the phone? I would also still like to speak with you if you could give me another telephone number and a time that is convenient. I am quite disturbed by what information I have on Centro Victoria.

I hope that you and your family have a lovely Christmas, and a much happier New Year.

Many thanks,

Kate (Osborne)

Hello Joseph   15 Deecember 2001

I cannot believe yet that all of this has happened. Is there any way that I can speak to you or you can contact me? I know it is really soon and probably cannot answer any of my questions. But I need to know:

How long your total programme is and what the different stages entail? (4 months seeing nobody, then visits on Sunday – for how long?)

How are you being treated – what is involved?

What conditions are you staying in? What is your room like?

How do you feel?

Do you want me to be in contact or not?

What will you do when you come out? Bali or Peru?

What are you thinking?

Is there no time that we can speak? Can you let me know anything through Lucia?

I picked up a lot of photos today – most are pretty ugly but I will send them anyway. Still waiting for Poca and the ones he can get. He promises all the time but never comes through. I am getting used to that being a real Latino trait!

I have had a brainwave and called the British Embassy in Lima. I spoke to a very nice lady who is getting me the number for drug rehab clinics there. She is sending me addresses and phone numbers by email within one hour (just call me Sherlock Holmes). Anyway, instead of having to wait I can call up myself and find out what the treatment is all about, how long, how you are 'reformed'(!) and just hear from the doctors that you are doing well every now and then. I can also find out if it is worth writing to you or sending things (i.e. if you are allowed to receive anything) Also if it is good or bad for you to have this contact with me...

If you want me to be here then we will see. If not, well, a relationship takes two and I understand that for your 'new life' you may not be able to be with me. Just let me know as soon as you can, however you can – and don't worry – I'm fine and will use this time positively I promise. Let's both get bigger, and better individually – and see if we can't be together again later.

It is the same night. I have just got back from the internet. I called a few clinics and have contacted a psychiatrist at a rehab clinic in Av. Las Artes. He speaks perfect English and has given me his private numbers and email. He has told me all about Centro Victoria. It sounds like a poor house, not a rehab place. He said that you would be praying six hours a day – which is great, the other things he said are not great. It sounds like a Catholic version of Hare Krishnas?

This psychiatrist, Luis, was not very complimentary about it – and that is an understatement. I know that you are there by choice, and I can only back your decision 100% if you are sure? Luis said that you will come out a different person, that you have to go out and sell candles to make money and that there are thousands of people there.

I know you are lost, and I know you are trying to find help and I want to help you do that, in any way I can – as a friend before a girlfriend. If you are sure that is the right place for you then good, but if not let's find somewhere else for you. Luis' place gives both psychiatric and psychological help. It is run a bit like the military giving you a very strict routine and rules. I feel it would be better suited to you. I am sure that you are gaining a lot in this time by speaking with God and centering yourself finding the right path again. A few weeks at Centro Victoria will do you no harm at all – we could all do with more spirituality in our lives and to be surrounded by people who are all seeking God and solitude is a very positive and powerful thing.

I feel that the photographs I planned to send are totally unsuitable for the journey that you are on. They were to have in the kind of institution I thought you were in – I did not realize you were on your way to becoming a monk! (Monk = male nun. Often living in silence and always in solitude). But it is your journey. I have to respect your decisions.

I love you

Kate X

Sadly there was little by way of religious conversion. Whatever benefits all those hours of prayer and spiritual contemplation brought about, it was very swiftly over-turned and Joseph was soon back to his old ways.

He returned to Bali in the spring of 2002, having written a series of letters to Kate, begging her to get him out of 'this hell-hole'. Unfortunately he also persuaded Kate to send him the money for the ticket from Peru, money which she did say he would have to repay when he could. He would later blame her for forcing him to abandon his attempt at rehabilitation.

While he was incarcerated in the Victoria Centre, Kate had been free to enjoy the friendship of western friends. She had some close girl friends and there were some married couples as well as mothers with children, whom she befriended. For a while she did some of the things women of her age normally do, had her hair done, got fitter, went out for a drink with friends and enjoyed her house.

On his return Joseph quickly reverted to type. He would go missing for one or two weeks at a time; surfing was the reason given. It transpired a while later that he was seeing other women and almost certainly in trouble with drugs. After one rather more prolonged 'surfing competition' Kate tracked him down to a nearby island where he was staying in a luxury hotel with a western woman. When he returned, he continued to live off Kate; money disappeared from her bank account, she was constantly paying off his debts and trying to keep him out of trouble.

During his frequent absences she was able to catch up with her own friends without the stress of trying to deal with this mad man, often high, increasingly violent and entirely unreliable, but whom she took back in spite of her own better judgement. She seems to have excused much of his behaviour because of their different cultures and no doubt he could still lie convincingly when he needed to.

When thrown out, which he was at intervals, she would meet her friends both male and female, but he would track her down and stand staring ominously at her. A number of the western men we later met testified to the fact that his behaviour was possessive in the extreme and even occasionally violent.

One man, whom Patrick and I met, liked Kate a lot and wanted to go out with her; Kate, although deeply unhappy with Joseph, said it wasn't the right time. The friend later told us it was all too threatening. Most of her friends found the Peruvians and Brazilians menacing, as did Kate, but she refused to be intimidated by them. There were constant dramas and scenes when they were around; shouting led to accusations and occasionally full-on fights. In her naivety, she remained convinced that if she could wean Joseph off the other 'Latinos', get him away from bad company, they could work it out. She was coming home in June and we were desperate to see her.

10

LAST VISIT

Kate came home in June 2002. There had been an acrimonious parting of the ways with Joseph before she left Indonesia, and she arrived home to depart almost immediately for her friend Lucy's wedding in the south. No one would have guessed what had been going on; we certainly had no idea how bad things were. She wasn't about to spoil her friend's wedding day and, strong as she was, Kate put on a brave face, caught up with old friends and put all the baggage of recent months behind her for a while.

However some days into her visit, she phoned Ketut the maid who looked after her home in Bali, to make sure Maizie was thriving. Yes, she was told her beloved Weimaraner was doing well, playing endlessly with the children and Helley, the household mutt. However, there was something 'very bad'. Joseph had been to the house stealing things. There was nothing Ketut or her husband could do to stop him.

Before she came home he had stolen money from his own kind, the Latinos, but was so terrified of the consequences he told Kate. Apparently he had 'used' money he owed to one of the senior bosses. Whether this was money he had been paid for couriering drugs or just money he borrowed to fund his own cocaine use it is difficult to know. Despite the fact that Joseph said he was terrified they would shoot him, Kate did not heed the inherent danger. She just saw it as a black and white situation where money had been borrowed, so it needed to be repaid. She took a considerable sum of money out of her savings as a 'loan' to Joseph, made him get into the car and drove him to repay his debtors. She waited in the car whilst he went into the house.

We did a lot of talking here at Black Dub. I was increasingly uncomfortable with the scenarios she was getting into. These were dangerous waters.

I can see her now in jeans and a jumper leaning against the Rayburn stove, cup of tea in hand. Her face looked haunted. She knew she had to make a decision about whether to stay on in Bali, without Joseph, or pack up and come home. Before she left in June she had demanded that Joseph pay back all the money she had lent him since she first met him – a considerable sum now. He assured her he would. Given that the debt ran to many thousands of pounds and Joseph wasn't working, I was at a loss to know how she thought he could achieve it.

It was a dreadful time. Kate felt there was nothing for her in Britain. A lot of her friends had moved on, buried themselves in their careers, got married, had children. She felt totally out of sync. I can see her now in the annexe going over and over what had happened in Bali with Joseph. She kept saying, 'What a mess I've made of things.' It was heart breaking.

I tried to build her up again – reminding her of all the things she was good at – design work, joinery, photography, writing (all those amazing letters I'd received). She could have made her living from any one of those. I pointed out what a much-loved daughter, sister, aunt and granddaughter she was. How much her friends valued her. We all missed her terribly. Unable to persuade her what a remarkable, talented person she was, I simply asked, 'Where would you be happiest?'

The answer came back with little hesitation – 'Bali'.

By the time she left Black Dub again she seemed clearer in her own mind and resolved to sort things out. Patrick and I, however, were concerned enough about the situation to insist that she should always get a return plane ticket and just leave the return part open. That way all of us would know she could escape if she needed to.

She was going to sever her ties with Joseph once and for all. This would prove to be much easier said than done. I believe, and notes written in the early stages of their relationship appear to substantiate this, that Joseph did love Kate, but the pressure of being in a relationship where the cultures were very different, with the demands it entailed if they were to make a long term commitment, were too much. He was surrounded by fellow countrymen, most of whom were connected to the drug world one way or another, and with his addictive history, it could never work.

Kate was naïve, too trusting; she didn't realize what she was dealing with. Her ignorance of the depth of his involvement with cocaine, coupled with the fact that she wanted to believe in him, meant she thought they could make it work and no one could persuade her otherwise. When she did realize that he and his companions were significant players in the drug trafficking network into and out of Bali, it was too late. Their relationship was doomed. Joseph would not allow her to get on with her life and date other men. He was not going to let her live in Bali without him, no matter how acrimonious it had become, and how monstrous his behaviour to her.

She returned to Bali in September and at first life was quiet; the break had done her good and we hoped had set her up, giving her the strength to deal with what she had to do – but we had little idea of the enormity of what she was dealing with.

Joseph appeared to have re-thought his approach, reappearing and assuring Kate he really loved her, wanted to be with her, and imploring her to take him back. Those other women she had accused him of having affairs with meant nothing to him. They were a distraction to take his mind off the fact that Kate did not love him anymore.

He promised everything would change and for a short while they were happy. He moved back into the house and they tried to make a go of things. The Latino friends were officially banned and they cooked and went out together like any normal couple.

But Kate wanted commitment and at least some of her money back. He was incapable of taking any responsibility. He accused her in one letter I've seen of 'only thinking about money' and 'being obsessed about the money'. Nothing could have been further from the truth. Money mattered little to Kate, it was just a means to an end, but Joseph was getting desperate. He came from a very different, intrinsically macho culture and didn't take well to headstrong women demanding what was rightfully theirs.

Kate was a feisty person and evoked passions that could, and did on occasion, spill over. She questioned him about the divorce which he often talked of, but which never materialized and the son, George, whom he never saw. She asked him what he was going to do for a living? When she got nowhere with this line of questioning, she threatened to go to Interpol with the names and telephone numbers of those friends of his she knew to be involved in the drug trade on the island.

He, on cocaine, would physically assault her. She wound up in hospital twice because of his violence, said she had slipped on some rocks. Ketut, the maid, who witnessed some of these incidents, told her to fight back, and she eventually did, but it was counter-productive. Joseph was taller and stronger than Kate; they were no match.

The girls always said as they grew older that I was wrong to urge them as children and in their early teens to turn the other cheek. They said I should have encouraged them to fight back when challenged. But strong and independent though she was, Kate did not countenance physical violence. She fought with words, not with her fists.

Once, in a fit of rage, Joseph destroyed her passport. When she went for an interview to get a replacement, the British Consul evidently read between the lines and realized she was in some domestic trouble. The Consul told her to come and see him personally if she had any more problems.

Early in October, Ruth and I were at a three-day event in Staffordshire, many miles from home, when my mobile phone rang. Ruth was competing pretty seriously by this stage and we spent a great deal of time out on the road with the horses.

It was Kate. Maizie was unwell, had a raging temperature and she was very concerned. Helley, the other dog in the house, had recently been poisoned and she was concerned that Maizie might have been targeted too. Please could I consult a vet on her behalf? There must be someone at Weston Park who could help? She sounded desperate, at the end of her tether.

Maizie was like a baby to Kate and I knew better than to suggest she went to see someone on Bali – she knew their opinion of dogs out there. But ask one of these vets! My initial thought was, I can't do that. Vets are like gods at these horse trials. Then I thought, they can only say no. Kate was very insistent, obviously distressed, and as it happened we were standing only a few feet from one of these minor deities who obligingly agreed to talk to my daughter when I explained the problem.

At three-day-events vets are pretty much run off their feet, on call throughout. I was a little embarrassed but everyone took it in good part. The fact that they were equine vets and not small animal specialists didn't seem to matter, as the advice he gave Kate was clearly good and we later heard that Maizie had made a good recovery from whatever the problem was.

At six in the morning on 13 October 2002 the phone rang. It was Kate again. 'Just to let you know I'm all right,' she said. We had no idea what she was talking about. She briefly explained that there had been a huge explosion in the middle of Kuta, in the tourist area; in a club she had often frequented. It had happened at 11pm on Saturday, the busiest time of the week. She sounded very shocked, said the streets were all burnt out around it, there were shells of cars and all you could hear were the sirens of ambulances and police vehicles. She would ring later. In the meantime we turned on the news to hear of the atrocity that was unfolding in Bali.

The Sari Club and Paddy's Bar, two very popular venues for Australian and international tourists in central Kuta, had been targeted. I remembered how often Kate had mentioned those names as places to which she had taken friends for a night out. Images of bloodstained and severely burnt young holidaymakers, struggling to escape the flames filled the screen. It was a scene of terrible carnage – blown-out buildings and charred remains. There were bodies everywhere. The Indonesian Chief of Police later said that the attack, primarily caused by a suicide bomber and a large car bomb, was the 'deadliest act of terrorism in the history of Indonesia'.

Kate and many others went to the Consulate – by now the British Embassy in Jakarta was also heavily involved – and they delegated tasks. Speaking fluent Indonesian, Kate was useful and worked tirelessly, like all the others, on some simply dreadful jobs. One of the things she was asked to do was to sift through the bombsite, identifying artefacts. I rang her every evening just to be on the end of a phone if needed. It was very shocking, depressing and exhausting. I have never heard her sound so low.

Amazingly Kate didn't lose any close friends in the bombings. But she knew many who did. Indonesian, Australian or British, the bomb had indiscriminately killed people whose only crime was that they were out relaxing and having a drink on a Saturday night. I could tell from her voice how shaken she was by what she had witnessed. Retrieving flip-flops and trainers, a tie-dyed scarf or embroidered purse containing pictures of family, it was just so close to home. Going out dancing or clubbing was much of Kate's enjoyment. It could very easily have been her.

When as many bodies as possible had been identified and personal effects gathered, Kate, because of her knowledge of the language, was asked if she would meet British relatives at the airport coming over to retrieve what they could. She couldn't do it – it was just too much. Eventually al Quaeda would claim responsibility for the Bali bombings which killed over 200 people and left hundreds severely injured.

The attacks were a terrifying indication that militant Islamic groups were hitting soft targets like nightclubs and bars rather than embassies and prominent buildings. In Kuta no one dared go out any more, particularly not to places where mixed crowds of tourists congregated, which essentially put the whole area off-limits. The terrorist action had frightened many westerners and almost all of Kate's friends left Bali. Prior to this there had been a large community of ex-pats who spent as many months as they could in this seemingly idyllic spot. Now that the terror threat had come to them, it was time to leave. Kate had been pursuing several interesting work leads, but there were no jobs available in the aftermath of the bombs. It was the most terrible blow to the tourist industry. She was very isolated.

I could hear how bad it was when we spoke on the phone, her voice betrayed her. She desperately felt the need to come home, especially with Christmas approaching, but with the mass exodus of westerners clamouring to get on the next flight out, was unable to get a ticket.

She did not mention Joseph any more. I think he sometimes did come back, but they were no longer an 'item'. She had a tenant, a Frenchman called Bruno Durrand, who paid his portion of the rent and so made living in her house more financially viable. I heard very little about him, just that she had put up adverts in and around Kuta and he had responded. In his thirties, he worked occasionally on the ferries travelling to and from the island. I was pleased to hear she had a small income and some company at this time.

She told me she had received a wonderful letter from the British Embassy thanking her for her help and contribution in the weeks following the atrocities. I have it in my possession now. It's a great reminder how much Kate could put aside any squeamishness or personal feelings and just get on with the job in hand, however unpleasant.

In the New Year of 2003, Kate made a decision to move back to England permanently; the last few months had taken their toll on her and she had made up her mind to come home. However, she couldn't just jump on a plane since she absolutely would not leave her dog Maizie. Everything else in her possession could either be packed up and shipped back or sold, but her dog was her constant companion, her child really, and she could not countenance leaving without her. We spent weeks on the phone trying to make a plan that would meet immigration requirements for the dog, but which would allow Kate daily access to her.

Eventually she asked if I could find quarantine kennels with the best reputation closest to Black Dub. And would I enquire whether she could park her camper van on the premises, working at the kennels? She didn't mind doing the most menial work for the minimum wage. That way she would be earning some money and seeing her beloved dog every day.

To this end, Kate herself had to have the rabies vaccination, which she did, and Maizie had all the necessary injections. We found kennels near Newcastle willing to cooperate, not too far from home. This took until April to organize, and of course we had not realized that after the dog had the rabies injection there needed to be an interval before a blood test could be taken to prove it had been effective. In all, the process would take six months. It was extremely laborious, time-consuming and expensive, but we told ourselves it would be worth it just to have the two of them back home again.

We still had to fix a date for their flight home. Kate had investigated which airline would be best suited to freighting Maizie, and she had a sizeable crate made for her through the vet on Bali. Kate had given English language lessons to the vet, and her doctor, on Bali in exchange for treatment for the dog and herself when necessary.

She phoned home for the third time in a week to confirm that she had seen the crate, it was well constructed, quite roomy, though Maizie had taken one sniff at it and turned up her nose. The next job was persuading her into it, but she was working on that. Now she was ready to make a booking with the airline. She just wanted to be totally sure the quarantine kennels were really okay about her parking the van up and living in. I said that surprisingly enough they were. In fact they had welcomed the idea – 'extra security on site'. It looked as though it could really work. All the vibes were positive. Kate and Maizie would be home before long.

PART TWO

Ruth and Kate, 1996.

11

SILENCE

Kate had gone silent. One week, two weeks, three weeks had passed without any word at all. I kept leaving messages on her answer machine. She had been complaining about the unreliability of her phone and talked of replacing it, but until now we had managed regular communication. We were talking to her once a week, more often while making plans for her homecoming and arrangements for her dog; the maximum we would leave it was ten days.

Three weeks had passed since we had last spoken about the crate and the kennel situation in Newcastle. That had been an entirely positive conversation, tying up the ends. We'd left it that she'd contact me as soon as she had the flight details.

At first I put it down to her erratic phone and knew she would ring us when she could. Into the third week I became worried, still leaving messages. Her mobile was switched on, so she, or someone, must have been charging it.

By the time Patrick and I went to supper with friends on the Saturday I was so worried that I mentioned to someone that I hadn't been able to contact her. Articulating my fears to someone else, a person outside the family, made it more real. Although the friend tried to placate me with the general unreliability of our grown-up children, I was unable to shake off the sense that things weren't right. I went home in a mild state of panic.

The following day, Sunday, we tried constantly and frantically to get hold of the Foreign Office, but got only an answer machine. On the Monday we were travelling as planned to Hampshire to stay with my sister and brother-in-law. Patrick drove as I tried to raise the Foreign Office, but it was the Monday of the Bank Holiday, and so we had more of the answer machine.

As soon as we got to Robert and Jen's we tried the Indonesian Embassy, also answered by a messaging service. In neither case were we given an emergency number to call. By now we were having to control our panic, and just did not know what to do.

Finally, the following morning, we raised the Foreign Office and expressed our extreme concern. They emailed the part time Honorary Consul on Bali, but of course there was a big time difference: they are seven hours ahead of us, so we had another agonizing wait.

When we got a reply from the Consul it was to say Kate had disappeared, last seen alive on the night of 18/19 April 2003. It was now 6 May. She was supposed to have dinner with a few western friends on Tuesday 22 April and, when she didn't appear, they went to see if she was all right. They were worried that she wasn't at home. Ketut, the maid, said she hadn't seen her since Friday night and she was looking after the dog who was very miserable. The friends reported her missing to the police and to the Honorary Consul, neither of whom thought of contacting us. The Consulate staff took away some of her personal possessions, and one of the staff took in Maizie. Apparently people go missing all the time for all sorts of reasons and they were not moved to explore further.

No words can describe the unimaginable horror into which we were being catapulted.

My brother-in-law Robert suggested that we contact his nephew, a detective in the drug squad in Sussex Police Force, working at Gatwick Airport. Although looking for missing people in foreign countries wasn't his brief, we had to start somewhere and there was the advantage that he was family. He and his senior officer were with us within two hours. I did my utmost to hold it together. It took all my strength and mental resolve to keep focused. Fortunately they were very professional, quickly up to speed with what Kate was doing on Bali, with her plans to return. They questioned Patrick and me separately about anything and everything to do with her life.

The officers, DC Mortimer Klein (known to the family as Mort) – a year older than Kate, he was 36 and had met her on several occasions – and Detective Sergeant Michael Smith, or Mick, as we quickly learnt to call him, said the most pressing thing was to piece together Kate's last known movements. They therefore contacted the Foreign Office, the Honorary Consul, the chief of Bali police and also the British Embassy in Jakarta, which they felt might have more resources than the part-time office in Bali.

The two constants were that we knew Kate would never go away without letting us know and that she would never abandon Maizie. Each of us said this repeatedly. Our daughter was in regular communication with us and she would have been in touch, even about a last minute plan to go away. And she would never have just left the dog; Maizie was everything to her.

It was thought best that Patrick and I got home to Cumbria, leaving the police to do the job they knew. They suggested that one way we could assist them was to phone and email every contact we could; friends, acquaintances, anyone who might be able to help. Unfortunately this was limited as we were unable to access Kate's email account, which had not been used since early April. She always kept her address book in her bag with her mobile phone. They were two of the most important things in her life. They went missing with her.

We spread the word as widely as possible and were absolutely swamped with replies. Kate's friends responded with immediacy and horror. Then we had to sort what might be relevant, prioritize and get communication running between those who could be helpful and the police.

There were records Kate had left on my computer when she was last home the previous summer and with those Hotmail accounts and others and with her friends around the world, most notably Jamie Sherriff and Francesca Fairbairn, her old friends from school days in Scotland, we managed to reach a lot of people. There were so many we would be grateful to over the coming months, and years, and ongoing. We made contact with school friends, colleagues from David Hicks, old design clients, friends from London, fellow backpackers the world over, people who'd stayed with us, ex-boyfriends, an old landlord – we racked our brains for anyone whom Kate might have got in contact with if she was in some kind of trouble.

We were so utterly out of any kind of comfort zone. It was completely unreal, except that it wasn't. We had to do as we were told. And do it to the best of our ability; and think, think, think of anything that might throw light on what had happened, and we did, day and night as we all felt absolutely sick with dread.

Had she mentioned any problems recently? Any financial worries? Had she mentioned any rows? Any domestic problems? My brain whirred, going over and over everything she'd said. We had heard little about Joseph for a while now. If anything it seemed there had been fewer problems of late. All our conversations had been about coming home.

We drove back up to Cumbria the following day. It was obvious we needed to be in our own space at this time. In coming home we were returning to the comfort of Christian, Ruth, Francis and the grandchildren, Poppy and Charlie. I felt so blessed that they were living at Black Dub at the time. They were an incredible strength for us; Christian with excellent secretarial skills, and her PA work, aided by Ruth, helped deal with the media. The two sisters kept the household going, while Ruth ran the yard and the horses. Francis with his computer skills set up a website to raise awareness that Kate had gone missing and a host of schemes for us when he was home at weekends; All three lent their wisdom and kept us sane. On a practical level there was a lot to keep us all occupied.

But in returning home we were leaving behind the presence of the two detectives who knew what was going on. They were based at Gatwick and couldn't be redeployed to Cumbria on a whim, however much we would have liked them to be. But we were fortunate. They had got the ball rolling and remained very much in touch during the handover period to our local police force, keeping us fully informed. Thank God for the computer. We are ever grateful to Mort Klein and Mick Smith for kick-starting the investigation and putting so much into it until it became impractical for them to continue.

Kate was a Cumbrian woman and as such came under the jurisdiction of Cumbria Police, apart from which, geographically, it made sense for them to take over.

We were terribly apprehensive about this situation. We had made a connection and had bared our souls to someone we knew, albeit in an official capacity. Mort and Mick were in charge as far as we were concerned, and it was frightening to have to start again. Could a police force in the far north of rural Cumbria offer as much help as two officers from one of the UK's busiest airports?

In the long run we need not have worried. The short term though was a different matter. On our return two police officers and a family liaison officer came out to go through everything on the strength of their brief from the Sussex police. We felt completely at sea; a liaison officer seemed an irrelevance – we had a job to do and needed direction.

The following day two senior officers came to see us. They took up the baton. Detective Chief Inspector Bill Whitehead and Detective Inspector Sean Robinson liaised with Sussex police until the moment came for them to head up the investigation. They were two exceptionally experienced officers, having spent many years in the fraud, murder and drug squads. They were business-like but friendly, didn't patronize us or beat around the bush. My first observation was that Bill Whitehead had the most piercing grey eyes I had ever seen, aged about 50. He was not particularly tall, was witty and had a dry sense of humour. He was also dynamic, incisive, forthright, not much would pass him by; I was glad he was on our side. Bill and Sean were a good foil for each other. Sean was well over six feet tall, about 40 and rather a gentle giant. From the North East, he had the traditional Geordie warmth, maybe not what you would expect from one of the most senior officers in Cumbria.

They took up and pursued the contacts with the Foreign Office, Embassy, Jakarta, Honorary Consul and all the leads we had made in the interim.

The 13 May, Kate's birthday, came and went. She would have been 35 years old. There was no news. Time was ticking away. I needed to bridge the 7,000 miles gap between us. I didn't want to fill in any more bits of paperwork or answer questions about her social life. I was desperate to see with my own eyes what had been going on. Any mother in my position would have wanted to do the same.

Patrick and I repeatedly asked when we could go to Bali. We were anxious to get out there as fast as possible, but Bill and Sean, as we came to know them, persuaded us not to go on our own as it was potentially dangerous ground, and we did not speak the language nor have any investigative skills. At this stage they were seeking permission from the Chief Constable to go to Indonesia, and of course they had to seek permission from the Bali Police to investigate a crime in their country. It was extremely delicate and had to be handled with the greatest diplomacy. If all this was granted, they urged us to be patient and go with them. They had a lot of groundwork to do before they could contemplate flying there, so as not to waste any valuable time once on the island. Their analysts were working daily on every piece of information coming in. It did not make good reading.

We, of course, just wanted to be where Kate was, and fast, but such were the persuasive powers, and common sense of Bill and Sean that we agreed to wait. Everything seemed to move at a snail's pace due to several factors; the time difference, the fact that the Honorary Consul was part-time with his own business to run and therefore didn't always pick up his mobile phone messages or emails and the fact that Balinese police rarely bothered to reply even when bombarded by email.

The police on Bali didn't actually go to Kate's house until 20 May. They did no forensics on either the house or her car, which had been found abandoned on 20 April at Denpassar Airport. The car had been cleaned and re-let for hire, destroying any possibility of finding any fingerprints or anything useful in terms of DNA. The car being discovered at the international airport did give us a glimmer of hope though. Was it possible she'd flown off at the last minute and was currently somewhere so remote there weren't any phones? It was a wild notion, something you allow yourself in times of desperation.

There was much to be done in the meantime. The priority was to find 'Joseph', otherwise known as Jose Henricci, Kate's one-time fiancé and on-off boyfriend, about whom there was all sorts of wild speculation. There was a rumour that he had flown back to Peru three weeks before Kate's disappearance. But there was other intelligence which put him much closer to what was beginning to look like the scene of a crime.

Jamie Sherriff had immediately got in touch with an old friend of his, Luli Orchard, who lived in Bali with her husband. Although she had never met our daughter, Luli made masses of enquiries and came up with quite an assortment of names and telephone numbers of people whom she personally did not know, but thought could be useful. She'd had quite a job, with so many of the westerners who had turned Bali into a second home having fled the island following the bombing. She kindly gave me a long list of telephone numbers which I proceeded to work my way through.

Of a very mixed bag, some knew Kate through the bars and cafes she frequented or the beach parties that were held quite often. They knew her socially. Although well meaning in most cases, they did not know her well, not as good friends do. They seemed a world away from her old friends from home Iona, Mairi, Jamie, Francesca or Lucy. But I had to shrug off any initial prejudices and listen to what they said. All knew of her relationship with Joseph. All were united in thinking he and his associates were bad news.

Unfortunately the rumour-machine and scaremongering were well under way, speculation rife and absolutely unbelievable – but terrifying for us. One story was that Joseph and Kate had run away to Peru, another that they had gone to Australia, another that he'd had a bad motorbike accident putting him in a wheelchair after coming off a remote mountain road in Peru; the detail wasn't spared.

Of course, Bali is a small island, a drama leads to gossip and rumour, especially amongst the ex-pat community. We heard some terrible theories about Kate. The police reassured us that they were being fed by the perpetrators of the crime. It was extremely distressing.

On the other hand I spoke at length on the phone to three Europeans who did know Kate. They said she had her head screwed on, stayed well away from the drug scene and was an 'exceptional person who would never do anything stupid'. They were very reassuring that Kate would not be mixed up with anything.

They too disliked Joseph. They did not think he would kill her, but confirmed that several times she had tried to leave him and he had pursued her until she took him in again. They had no idea what had happened to her, but felt it was not good, and quite possibly had something to do with the Peruvians. All these people were clear about one thing: the Peruvians were hated because they were thought to be above the law.

The government, police and army were not to be trusted; money talked. The drugs industry was worth millions of dollars in Indonesia, particularly on the party island of Bali. Bribes and back-handers were routinely paid to officials in government, the legal system and the prison service. Despite the threat of the death penalty for drug trafficking and occasional high-profile crackdowns on the perpetrators, drugs were rife on the island. The more I heard, the more I began to feel worryingly out of my depth.

With Luli Orchard's list to hand I rang Bali constantly, talked to as many people as I could, to see if there was any consensus. One minute I would feel I was getting somewhere, the next I was back where I'd begun. Very fortunately, as I related each and every phone conversation to Bill and Sean, repeating the awful unbelievable stuff that was being said, they put a perspective on it, calming my panic. They said they did not deal in rumour, only in facts, and they doubted whether any of this was based on more than gossip or conjecture.

We were meeting with the police frequently, and were advised to go about our daily lives, keeping our mobiles on us at all times. This was obviously extremely difficult to do, but we tried. Focusing on anything other than Kate was well nigh impossible.

Patrick was desperate and finding it difficult to deal with the enormity of what was going on. I felt I had to be on the ball at all times. Whereas before I would have had a glass of wine or two with supper in the evenings, now I drank less and often not at all. For the first time in my life I drank coffee throughout the day and into the night. I had to keep myself alert.

I frequently stayed up very late, sitting on the sofa in the sitting room going over and over things. Christian or Ruth would join me and we would talk into the small hours. When I got emotional, the girls stayed so strong. They were a tower of strength. Christian had always been the independent one of the three. Now, she sat and listened and made wise comments. Most importantly she gave me great hugs when there was nothing else to say.

In the meantime, life had to go on. Ruth had entered her horses for some competitions, having made her plans for that year as one does – usually starting on plan A and winding up on D or even Z – and we made an attempt to stick to it. The eventing season was well under way and she had an intermediate horse and two youngsters all doing rather well.

We took all three to Bishop Burton near Hull. Ruth said she was going into this competition for Kate, determined to do well. The youngsters were very pleasing, and the older horse was lying second before the cross-country. He went clear which would have meant he'd moved up and won his class; however, Ruth was oblivious to the fact that she'd jumped an advanced jump by mistake – not too difficult as they were all in a fence line – and she was eliminated. We both broke down in the lorry, letting go of a great deal. We knew we could not go on eventing for the time being. It's a dangerous sport and demands complete focus. It was to be the last event Ruth competed in.

Ruth had her own trauma to deal with. The older sister whom she loved, had looked up to, admired, partied with, backpacked round Bali with, was missing. The police had quizzed her at length in case she had any information from her sister that I, as her mother, might not have been aware of. Bill and Sean kept warning me that they might uncover aspects of Kate's life which she had kept hidden from me. Over the years personal letters had gone back and forth between the girls – perhaps one of these would shed some light on her mental state? Ruth duly handed them over but there was nothing, no inkling, that she might have been about to disappear. The process for Christian and Ruth, as for all of us, was unbelievably gruelling.

Joseph had to be found. It seemed too much of a coincidence that he too had gone missing. The police advised us the best way to achieve this was to use the media, and a series of television, radio and newspaper interviews were arranged.

For us, living in a rural community, quietly and privately getting on with day-to-day life, the idea of drawing attention to ourselves was anathema and quite terrifying; but if it was going to help it had to be done. Before it was mentioned at school, seen on television, or newspaper or heard on the radio Francis explained to Poppy and Charlie, as simply as possible, that Kate was missing. They were ten and eight years old and did not miss much.

Bill and Sean and their team were with us throughout, guiding us through the minefield of dealing with the press, teaching us how to field potentially difficult questions and getting the press on side. They advised us how to get our message across clearly, without appearing distant and cold or breaking down and losing the plot. Easier said than done when you're in a small room with countless journalists and cameras focused on you, recording your every move.

Our local television and radio were very empathetic and handled interviews sensitively, and the press conferences were pretty good. Naively, given hindsight, I thought there were some decent people there – anyway, they were not too intrusive. It was sympathetic and constructive.

Francis thought it could be a good idea to set up a website for Kate; very simple, photographs, a brief description, the date she went missing, when she was last seen. Bill and Sean thought it could be helpful, but warned us we were opening ourselves up to possible cranks and undesirables. Francis duly set it up and we did have numerous 'sightings' reported which eventually proved to be unfounded. It did have a lot of 'hits'. Francis also set up a fax and extra phone lines to deal with the constant calls from friends and a huge number from the press which Christian and Ruth fielded.

Bill and Sean had taken away my computer to get at the hard drive in order to access Kate's most recent email records from her visit home the summer before. Their analysts trawled through the emails: only one really caught their attention. It was a list of names and telephone numbers of people who she believed to be involved in smuggling drugs into Bali. The names were all Latin-American sounding and they included Joseph Henricci. She had sent it to Interpol. When they told me I felt sick. Kate had turned whistle-blower? I had to admit it wouldn't be out of character.

The next stage was to access her own email account, the one she frequently used from Bali. In spite of help and requests from extremely well connected people in Microsoft in America, which went as far as the FBI, we failed.

There was another serious consideration. Gran, Patrick's mother Dorothy, was used to my visiting her in the nursing home twice a week – fortunately never on specific days, but as and when I could. This dropped down to once a week and was one of many painful ordeals.

We decided as a family that we should not let Gran know anything about what was happening; possibly when things were resolved, but not for now. Kate was, after all, her favourite granddaughter. It was much better that she didn't start worrying and getting fretful. Ruth did remark 'but when Gran dies, won't it come as a shock to find Kate up there?' The staff at the home were wonderful and cooperated in ensuring she never had a paper or access to television, if something was going to be aired. It was actually very helpful that she was slightly losing the plot, couldn't operate the radio and couldn't work the remote control for the television.

However, the constant theme, where she had no lapse of memory, was on the subject of Kate. She adored her, hadn't had a letter in a while, and every single time I visited her she asked me, 'When is Kate coming home?' and I had to lie, pretend everything was fine and reassure her that Kate would be home before too long.

On the whole the press were sensitive. There is always an exception. I took a call one morning from a journalist working for one of the more reputable Sunday papers. After a brief preamble he told me he was standing outside Kate's house near Kuta. I was completely taken aback. He was there in Uluwatu! It didn't seem right. Why wasn't the house cordoned off anyway? Why were the press allowed anywhere near it?

I tried to contain the annoyance I felt with the Balinese authorities, who were supposed to be investigating a crime. He then went straight into questions – very direct and designed to throw me – about Kate. She had two passports – why? I couldn't think. I didn't know the answer till later when I discovered that Joseph had defaced her passport and her replacement passport, which was always in her handbag, had disappeared with her. When I suggested the journalist ring the police press office, which we had been advised to do, he didn't like it at all. 'Well, if that's the way you want to play it' were his words, and we were cut off. I didn't want to play at all.

I put the phone down and immediately called Bill Whitehead who remarked that this journalist appeared to be on a crusade. He too had received a phone call and felt that he was raking around, trying to scrape together the most sensational story possible. When I told Christian he might possibly ring back, she said she would deal with it and I was not to answer the phone. The girls were very protective of me.

The press interviews achieved the desired objective. Once the media machine started rolling it was broadcast all over the world. It was very strange to see the picture we had supplied of a smiling Kate at a dance in Cumbria, appearing in so many publications, in so many languages.

We had our first significant breakthrough when a friend of a friend contacted a colleague working in Mexico, who had formerly worked in Peru, Joseph's home country. With his help and that of journalists in South America we discovered Joseph's whereabouts. He was in a notorious prison on the Brazil/Peru border, awaiting trial in Lima for smuggling drugs. He had been arrested at Puerto Maldonado, five hundred miles east of the capital, with an unspecified amount of cocaine. He was facing a long prison sentence.

This led to so many other questions. When had he left Bali? Had he been around the night Kate disappeared? Would Kate have known of this smuggling operation? Again, there were so many conflicting reports: people who said they had seen him in Uluwatu the night Kate disappeared, or who had seen him at her house. Others said he had not been around for some weeks. It was difficult to know what to believe. The police were dealing with the most tricky circumstances, the cultural and political diversity between two countries – Britain, and Indonesia – with a certain key player now discovered in police custody in Peru. There were also different protocols and priorities. For those reasons the British police were not empowered to step in and direct the enquiry and had no control over how the Balinese police might respond. Finally, after more than two weeks of constant and insistent requests the British had received permission from the Indonesian Government and the Balinese police to assist with the investigation. It was the go-ahead we had been awaiting for so long.

We planned to fly there leaving on Sunday 14 June for two weeks. Bill and Sean, their team and analysts were working round-the-clock collating information, to be as fully prepared as possible for the task ahead.

My sister, Jen, came to stay the week before we were to leave. Like it or not I had to shop for a few basics in Carlisle, and I had lost the confidence to go on my own. We went together and I think Jen was quite astonished when strangers recognized me, touched my arm and wished me good luck. I was deeply moved and I was to become accustomed to it. For us, this has come to typify the Cumbrian community. Their thoughts and prayers, the depth of feeling, have sustained us during the initial pain of Kate's disappearance and have continued to do so.

At supper that evening I thanked Jen and Robert for everything they had done. Sisters and brothers-in-law don't come better than those two. From the time we first knew something dreadful had happened to Kate they pulled out every stop they could to help. On a practical and emotional level they were marvellous. Their wonderful sense of perspective and good humour kept us from losing the plot completely. Most importantly they loved Kate.

A very necessary form of sustenance for me during that awful time was to visit a local church. It didn't matter which, but St Martin's in Brampton fast became a favourite. Back then, it wasn't locked: you could just walk in as and when you needed to. I would spend anything from five to twenty minutes there. I was nearly always on my own. I wasn't expecting a miracle. I asked for strength as a family. I also went to St Cuthbert's Church in Carlisle, another lovely place. It never failed to restore calm and still does.

We were urged by a friend to meet John Aglionby, a journalist based in Jakarta, who had considerable experience of life in Indonesia. He was the South East Asian correspondent for *The Guardian*. About the same age as Kate, he was Cumbrian by birth and his mother lived locally. He was making a whirlwind visit home and kindly managed to see us over breakfast at seven thirty in the morning, a few days before we left for Bali.

He advised us as to how to conduct ourselves and what was form in Indonesia and what was not. He also spoke to Bill Whitehead about how best to deal with their police officials. We were grateful for his advice. He said we should keep in touch and that we might meet up in our hotel on Bali.

On Sunday 14 June Ruth drove us to Manchester Airport where we met Bill and Sean who had been driven from Carlisle by their wives. In the hope of finding Kate we were carrying a few photographs she had wanted of Ruth's horses and photos of the children which Christian and Ruth had put together.

As we left Ruth at the airport, we were pretty choked, just as we had been when we left Christian and the children, and Jen at Black Dub. There had been a big team behind us in Cumbria, a large network all focused on one thing – finding Kate. Walking through to the departure lounge, we felt very alone.

It took more than 24 hours and a change of planes for us to reach our destination. As we flew over Bali I hated the place, but we had to see where Kate lived and see something of the island she had once loved and we prayed that in the short time we were there we would find some answers.

12

BALI INVESTIGATION

I kept a diary while on Bali and for some time afterwards. All my notes were hastily jotted down in a green hard-backed notebook. In order to keep Christian and Ruth informed we phoned them every day.

Monday 16 June

We arrived in Bali via Kuala Lumpur. It felt the longest plane journey I'd ever taken. I was sure Kate was dead, as was Patrick. We both felt it. The main thing was to find her body, find out what happened and bring her home. We were already exhausted. Walking through immigration at Denpassar airport, a huge scarlet sign accosts you; 'Warning! Death penalty for drugs traffickers.' It sets a rather menacing tone which heightened my sense of foreboding.

We were met by Mark Wilson, the Honorary Consul on Bali, who seemed nice enough. We also met the Orchards, Luli and Charles, who had been doing lots of groundwork prior to our arrival. Much the same age as Kate, they live permanently on Bali and had worked hard at setting things up for us – producing a list of the various police involved on the island as well as useful contacts who knew, or knew of, Kate. It was Luli who had furnished me with the list of telephone numbers of people who knew my daughter, many of whom I had called from the UK. They had also fixed us all up in the Intercontinental Hotel in Jimbaran.

Charles Orchard immediately took me to one side and asked me if I was happy with the way the British police were conducting the investigation. If I wasn't, he had contacts who could help. I reassured him that we were more than happy with the way Bill and Sean were conducting their investigation, but thanked him for the suggestion. It might be something we would need in the future.

Bill and Sean had a meeting straight off the plane with the Balinese police, which was not too encouraging. They were told that if they did their own thing and put a foot out of line, they would be deported. They were to be assigned an officer in the Balinese police force to take them around – in other words, they were to be shadowed. It was not going to be easy for them to do their work. In fact it was made difficult beyond belief.

We had dinner that first night with Bill and Sean. I still could not tell you where the hotel was or what it really looked like. After dinner I had a chat with John Aglionby, *The Guardian* correspondent with whom we'd had breakfast back home. It was good to see a familiar face, particularly someone with a link to Cumbria. Although, as Bill reminded me, John is a journalist, he did seem to care.

He had done some research since our earlier meeting. He had been to Kate's house and talked to Ketut, the maid. Again I felt irritation that a journalist had free access to my daughter's home, but I just had to bite my tongue. Ketut apparently saw Kate and Joseph leave together on the night of 18 April, which was hugely significant. It was the first time someone with a direct link to Kate had said Joseph was on the island on the night of her disappearance. Surely a journalist of his standing on a reputable paper wouldn't get that wrong?

The following day we were going to Kate's house to talk with the maid.

Tuesday 17 June

We were introduced to Tri, the Indonesian policeman who would be accompanying us. Patrick, Bill, Sean and I were all conscious we would have to work very hard to be welcoming and friendly to Tri. We had discussed this beforehand and all agreed that it was essential to get him on side. He was small in stature and short on personality. Totally inscrutable: when we had lunch with him and Bill and Sean later in the day there was absolutely no expression on his face throughout. Because he was our police shadow he came to Kate's house with us, witnessing a lot of emotional turmoil, but as usual there was no interaction.

I rang Luli to arrange a meeting with her 'contacts', some of whom had been at the same club as Kate, the night of 18 April. I wanted to speak with the people who had last seen her. Had they noticed anything strange? Did she seem apprehensive? Nervous? Did she mention going away?

At 8.30 we had breakfast with Bill and Sean. The assistant consul arrived from Jakarta, after which we were allowed to go through Kate's personal items, those things which had been removed from her house by the Foreign Office. These included her camera, numerous documents, telephone numbers etc. There was no passport or address book, those things were missing with her. It felt good to see some tangible possessions/signs of my daughter, but odd to be going through her things under those formal circumstances with the consul watching our every move.

A photographer from the Press Association came to take pictures. I tried to engage in conversation with the consul, who was Irish, but he was deeply uninspiring. The interpreter, whom we would need for our interviews with Balinese speakers, arrived. Her name was Gilda and she appeared to be Chinese, though perhaps not; it was difficult to tell. She was very nice.

We travelled in a four-wheel drive car for what felt like an interminable journey to get to Uluwatu, where Kate's house was. We had real trouble finding it, there were no signs, impossible to tell where one road started and another ended. Eventually we found it down a long track. I had seen so many photos of her home: it seemed very familiar. It was very compact. We went in through the doorway and there was a statue of Buddha in the garden.

And suddenly there was Ketut – the maid. She was tiny, quite young and attractive, dressed in western clothes. Through the interpreter she said, 'I've been waiting for you.'

We hugged each other for a long time – it was deeply emotional. She was clearly distressed; we clung to each other crying. She hugged Patrick too. But I couldn't allow myself to give in to my feelings for too long. We were all worried about breaching Indonesian protocol, doing something out of turn, mis-judging the emotion. Ketut's husband hovered in the background nervously. They were clearly both intimidated by their own policeman.

The house resonated Kate: amber, lavender and patchouli, the very essence of her. There was a slate board in the kitchen, and there in her distinctive hand, some memos: Write to Robert – his father had just died – Card to Gran, a list of telephone numbers, Arrange cargo for Maizie; an unopened letter from Lucy, her old friend at David Hicks, was propped on a kitchen surface.

Through Gilda our translator, I asked Tri if I could speak to Ketut. We needed all the help we could get from her and I was prompted throughout by Bill. It was such an important conversation I could not get it wrong and put her off talking or opening up. It was initially emotional. I gripped her hand and asked if she would do anything to help find Kate. She agreed. We sat down side by side holding hands. I asked a lot of questions through the interpreter. Was Joseph there on the night she went missing? No, the answer came back through Gilda. Joseph was emphatically not there in April, not seen at all before Kate's disappearance. So John Aglionby of *The Guardian* got that wrong?

On 18 April, the last night she was seen alive, Kate was very happy. She dressed up to go out. She said she was 'going to get her money back.' She did not say how. Ketut was not sure where she was going, but knew that she was meeting friends.

Ketut was surprised when she didn't come back that night or the next day because it was unlike her to leave Maizie. She became genuinely worried a few days later when the dog food ran out.

We left at two in the afternoon after three hours of questioning. It was clear that Kate had a good relationship with her maid, that the two women genuinely cared for one another, though it was obviously a boss/employee scenario rather than one of confidantes, as I would have expected. We hugged tightly again when I left. Ketut was a mother herself, albeit of much younger children, and she had the warmth of a mother. I trusted her.

I took a pink cotton top from Kate's wardrobe to keep with me. It smelled of her. She bought it in England. I broke down with Patrick and the team when we were back in the car. It was all too much.

We had a snack lunch though I could hardly eat. We all went to the car hire place where Kate had rented her vehicle, but infuriatingly it was closed, in common with many businesses in the afternoon. Patrick and I lay down exhausted only to be woken by the phone ringing. It was a request from Radio 4 to do an interview with James Naughtie of the *Today* programme. We decided that if it would help we would do it. In fact, Patrick did the talking.

Gilda asked for an interview, as, besides being a translator, she was also a presenter on the local TV channel. Although both Patrick and I felt this was a bit of a clash of interests, we clearly needed to raise the profile of our case in Bali and so we agreed. At least Gilda should have the advantage of being up to speed on the case.

Bill and Sean learned, after much abuse about his driving, that our driver spoke English. He was probably a plant!

The Guardian correspondent, John Aglionby arrived. He had been to Kerobokan jail in the heart of Kuta to interview a couple of inmates – Rodriguez Mascarenhas and Stephen Tower. Bali police made a gesture after the fuss about Kate's disappearance, arresting a few people for possession of drugs, but certainly none of the important ones and notably no Peruvians. They were arrested carrying small quantities and were easy targets. That was a preliminary meeting and John was going back tomorrow to speak further to Rodriguez who said he was 'very worried about Kate', but that was all. John was going to ask him about his contacts. Apparently the jail is squalid, rat-infested and disease-ridden.

Any mention of drugs made me feel defensive immediately. Because of Kate's relationship with Joseph Henricci, someone known to be dealing cocaine, it seemed she was assumed guilty by association. Bill and Sean had made a very professional search of her house and to my relief found absolutely nothing, not a trace of drugs, and they are highly trained in that area.

At 9.15pm Bill rang an ex-pat called Teresa, who was absolutely hysterical, making no sense. As the partner of Ronald, a Brazilian member of the Bali mafia, her name kept cropping up. She appeared to be quite loopy. An arrangement was made for the police to go and see her on Thursday at 9.30am. Teresa was British and had bought up properties on Bali over the last few years. Kate had referred to her as completely mad, after initially being grateful to have met another compatriot.

Patrick and I went down to the hotel restaurant to eat. Again we asked for a table away from everyone else. I didn't trust myself not to break down. Bill and Sean went out for a walk.

The next day, Wednesday, was to be a busy day. We were going to Luli Orchard's house to meet contacts of Kate, some of whom were the last people to see her on that Saturday night. Then Bill and Sean were meeting up with Lee Dixon, a senior Australian police officer. We were clearly going to need some international co-operation if we were going to get anywhere. Australia, being much closer geographically to Bali, might be able to help us navigate the minefield of protocol and bureaucracy on the island.

Mike Smith, the Cumbrian police press officer, called from England to say that contact has been made with Lima. We were a step closer to Joseph.

Wednesday 18 June

We had breakfast with Bill and Sean. While we were dining alone the previous night, they had gone into Kuta to a bar recommended by the Indonesian police. As they approached the bar, a man asked 'You like coke?' Bill did a double-take, thought he must have mis-heard, 'Sorry, what?' The man with his hand in his pocket repeated, 'You want coke?' 'No thanks' came the reply. He obviously didn't realize he was talking to a British drug squad detective!

At 10.30am we went to Luli and Charles Orchard's to meet some of the locals. It was so considerate of them to let us meet people in their house and not have to do it in the hotel or in the public surroundings of a café which would undoubtedly have inhibited conversation. They were a disparate collection. All were interesting, but in their own way, bizarre. It was possibly quite intimidating being interviewed by British police officers. Certainly it was rather formal and tense. I kept thinking – were these really the people she hung out with? There was something of the lost soul about them all. I was reminded once again how much patience Kate had for the waifs and strays of this world. I was also aware, for the first time, that some people seemed to have ghoulishly attached themselves to Kate since her disappearance, some of these 'contacts' seemed to be making a rather casual friendship go a long way.

One woman, Jenny, who runs the Woodstock bar, said she and her husband Eric, felt that Kate was a bit lonely which surprised me. Apparently one night she had said to them 'How do you make friends?' I could only put this out-of-character remark – if accurate – down to the mass exodus of westerners after the bombings. I warmed to Jenny more than most, but I didn't feel she knew Kate very well either.

When questioned about Kate's drug use, they said she would take recreational pot, but never anything heavy. One of the more articulate of the group said Kate was very upset that Joseph was having an affair with a married Swedish woman and that she was going to confront her and her husband. It was the first we had heard of this and it may have been just gossip or it may have been something more.

Bill and Sean were not convinced by any of these people; in fact they felt that bringing them all in had 'amounted to nothing'. Bill thought that what we had heard was 'by and large rubbish'. He was coming round to the idea that there was no drug involvement, no conspiracy, no Peruvian mafia. Perhaps something more spontaneous, domestic, a row that got out of hand?

It was becoming imperative to speak to Bruno Durrand, the Frenchman. He had rented Kate's spare room and was much around at the time of her disappearance, but had vanished into thin air. We had recently heard that he had been found a couple of days later very drunk and distressed. He had been badly beaten up, was covered in cuts and bruises and all the signs indicated that he knew something or had seen something. Emphasis was starting to shift from Joseph and the Peruvians.

At 4pm we did an interview for Bali TV which was farcical. Gilda worked through a list of questions for Patrick and then the identical questions for me, so the same ones were asked twice. I felt like a puppet in a show. At 6.30 Bill and Sean left for dinner with Lee Dixon, the very senior Australian policeman.

At 10pm that evening a woman rang thinking she had seen Kate on a website in Australia. This was quickly checked (the power of the computer), but turned out to be wrong. Unfortunately though in the brief moments while it was still a wild possibility, I felt my hopes rise.

Thursday 19 June

First thing in the morning we paid another visit to Kate's house to see Ketut, once again accompanied by Tri, the Indonesian policeman. He was there to observe us and to make sure we didn't step out of line, rather than to investigate a crime.

There was little to say to Kate's maid on this occasion that hadn't been said the first time around. Still I felt that same strong connection with her. I was sure she would tell me something if there were anything to say. It was definitely much better to be at the house than sitting at the hotel waiting for the phone to ring.

There was the question of rent. Kate last paid on 18 April. There had been no transactions on her bank account of any sort. We decided to extend the lease until 25 June. We pursued the line of enquiry about Bruno the lodger to try to establish absolutely whether he was there on the night in question. Ketut said no to Friday and Saturday, but he did return on Sunday.

I tried to take more in – the furniture, the special possessions – with a view to packing it up and sending it home. It was very hard to be practical when so much was up in the air. Once again, just being in Kate's house was very emotional for me. I had to stay focused during this process, but the mere sight of her things and her handwriting, choked me. I said a fervent prayer to Buddha in the garden. Patrick and I returned to the hotel.

Bill, Sean and Tri went to the office/shop from where Kate rented her mobile phone. Tri's commander had ordered them to get into her account. Tri had been told this case had priority and to get it sorted. Despite such instructions they were still unable to gain access to her phone records. In fact it would take until the last day of our stay in Bali to see a transcript of calls made and received on her phone.

Patrick went to Denpassar International Airport to sort out Kate's return ticket, but was told by a man at Royal Brunei Airlines that he had seen Kate buy a ticket in the last month. He said he would go through the records and would let us know tomorrow. Bill thought it was utter nonsense. Anyway, her ticket remained open till September.

I went through all of Kate's paperwork meticulously. There were copies of handwritten letters to Joseph which he had obviously returned to her. She, or someone, had torn some of them into lots of bits, but oddly, kept the pieces. I painstakingly sellotaped them together. One of Kate's letters to him raised the subject of his debt to her. By this stage it stood in excess of £20,000 and was clearly an issue between them. He accused her of 'only caring about the money'.

She accused him of not caring enough. It was distressing to read her sadness. Kate obviously knew that he had other women. While there was nothing directly relevant, the letters did bear out the tempestuousness of their relationship and the rumour that Joseph had been playing away and that Kate was going to confront him with it, as well as the other parties involved.

Bill and Sean talked to Cameron, a very engaging Australian, but like so many people on Bali, he was totally disorganized. Said he spoke to Kate on Saturday 19 April at noon, briefly, though Bill and Sean were not convinced he knew what day it was. He said the 'Woodstock lot' – the crowd associated with the club where Kate went on her last night, some of whom were part of the group we originally interviewed – were always trying to think of the next big drama. They had nothing better to do.

Bill and Sean went to see a contact of Luli, Philip Conway, who 'must speak' with Bill. Bizarrely he had absolutely nothing to say. It was infuriating. We were dogged by people like this, who just wanted to make themselves part of the investigation.

Patrick and I read in the garden of the hotel and then walked along the beach. There was a pool at the hotel and, although both of us are keen swimmers, we didn't go in. In fact we didn't swim in the pool once while we were there. We weren't there for a holiday. Bill and Sean got back at 7.45pm, frustrated and exhausted.

Friday 20 June

We contacted the Honorary Consul on Bali, Mark Wilson. Given Kate's work for the Consulate over the Bali bombing, I would be interested to see what he and his colleagues had to say, what memories they had of her.

In the meantime I had to be practical about the need to pack up Kate's possessions. I had to find a stationery shop. Did such a thing exist on Bali? All I had seen were endless shops selling puppets, wooden carvings and brightly-coloured ikat sarongs. Perhaps in the business area of Denpassar I would find the sticky labels and strong packaging materials I needed. I would make an inventory at the house and organize shipping. At least that was something to focus on.

Bill and Sean picked up Tri at 10am go to the airport. The Royal Brunei man found no booking for Kate after all. The immigration department was uncooperative even by Indonesian police standards and the computers didn't talk to each other; another dead-end.

Bill and Sean then went to the car hire place which turned out to be another impossible place to find, no street names, little lanes and alleys or 'gangs' everywhere. When they eventually tracked it down they discovered that the ticket left on the car at the airport had been burned and the car cleaned and re-let. Apparently it was left on 20 April according to the ticket.

Tri, the policeman, offered hookers to Bill and Sean. Would they have liked some pretty Balinese girls? When they politely said 'No thank you, we're married,' Tri replied 'So am I!'

Finally I got a chance to have a long talk with Mark Wilson, the Honorary Consul. Everyone who had met Kate liked her. Of course it was nice to hear good things about my daughter, particularly after so much negativity, but I felt he was being candid, opening up with me now, which was refreshing.

We talked about the dog. Mark told me that one of the embassy staff, Marie Claire, had taken in Maizie. I needed to go and visit her. Before I left England, Christian, Ruth and I had discussed the feasibility of bringing the dog back. The girls would very much have liked me to do so if possible. I needed to assess her new living arrangements and make a decision.

We had been invited to the Orchard's house for dinner that night and had rather apprehensively accepted. I didn't know whether it was a good idea. I hardly felt up to social chit-chat, but as everyone kept telling us – life must go on. Patrick and I took a taxi to buy wine for our hostess, Luli – it was very expensive and there was no selection. On our return we nearly had a diplomatic incident when Patrick said we paid 480,000 rupiah (approximately £30) for the cab. If so, we had apparently been seriously ripped off. Patrick had made a mistake which we did put right, but not before the poor taxi man was summoned by the security director! I grovelled, apologized profusely, horrified by how quickly small domestic incidents could escalate here. We must not put a foot wrong.

When I had a quiet time to myself I went through the paperwork I had taken from Kate's house on Thursday, piecing together some more of the letters. In them she poured her heart out to Joseph. It was very tough to read them, but I had to, in case they contained some clue to her whereabouts. Not only would she be mortified if she knew I had seen them, I found it almost unbearable that she could send such eloquent, beautiful letters to someone so undeserving. I didn't share them with Patrick.

After a late lunch, we walked along the beach, read in the garden and got ready for dinner with Charles and Luli Orchard. I was glad we made the effort to go. There was fish pie and interesting company. An architect, an explorer, a singing teacher – they restored my faith in human nature, which had been starting to flag. A lovely and illuminating evening. It was nice temporarily to think about something other than our missing daughter. Charles gave me his copy of *Love in a Cold Climate* by Nancy Mitford. I was very low on light reading. Christian and Ruth ensured I had plenty of their recommendations on leaving home, but I was reading myself to sleep, till about 4am most nights, and getting through them quickly.

Francis, our son-in-law, rang to say Bill couldn't get through to us. Lima was ringing in at 8pm.

We got back to the hotel about 11.15pm. Bill and Sean arrived back from supper out. Bill had a long talk to Graham Ballantyne at the embassy in Lima. Jose Henricci, or Joseph, who is currently going by the name of 'Zubiate' had been in prison near the Brazil/Peru border since 14 May. He was arrested trying to leave Peru via Puerto

Moldanado carrying more than four kilos of cocaine. He was looking at a very long prison sentence – more details tomorrow we hoped.

Joseph's brother, Jorge, who was a lawyer, was prepared to act as a conduit between his brother, the embassy and us as long as there was no media circus. We wouldn't tell the press, but, if past experience was anything to go by, it wouldn't be long before they were on to it anyway. Joseph's father was very ill; they didn't want him to know anything.

Eventually we got to bed about 2am. Everyone was exhausted. We agreed to have a later breakfast tomorrow.

Saturday 21 June

We met sometime after 9am for breakfast, to discover that Bill and Sean had had no sleep whatsoever. Charles, our host of the previous night, rang, somewhat the worse for wear, just after 2am. He told them that Bruno Durrand, the French lodger who had been eluding them, was at the Woodstock Bar. The suggestion was that they would all go over to the bar together to have a little talk with him. Bill and Sean were in a difficult position. They were under strict orders that visiting police officers were not allowed to hassle in someone else's country. It was out of hours and they did not have Tri, their 'shadow' with them. Such a meeting had to be by invitation only.

Charles Orchard argued persistently. At 4am the situation was resolved when Charles and Lucien arrived at the Intercontinental Hotel with Bruno, having decided to bring the Frenchman to Bill and Sean. I missed all of this, but apparently Bruno was reasonably sober and fit and was described as 'too pretty to be violent!' He was very emotional, clearly liked Kate, rented the room from her for one month and was now desperately worried about her. He didn't go to the house the night of 18 April.

Bill and Sean eventually got to bed at 6am. We breakfasted, everyone was tired. The police went back to their various rooms to try to get some rest for an hour. I took a call from the same journalist, Tim Sheridan, who had hassled me before with questions aimed at discrediting my daughter. Did I know that Kate had more than one passport? The answer to that was – yes. I had since ascertained from Mark Wilson, the Honorary Consul, that Kate had two passports because she'd had to renew her passport after Joseph had defaced it in a fit of rage. Tim Sheridan asked me if I thought that Kate was involved with drugs. As Bill had said, he was on something of a crusade. I repeated what Bill and Sean said after they'd searched Kate's house from top to toe, 'No evidence of drugs whatsoever'. And I pointed out to the man from *The Sunday Times* that they were not a couple of rural bobbies. They were two high ranking police officers, both of whom were used to turning houses inside out to find the slightest trace of narcotics. Some journalists scarcely think about checking their 'facts' before printing them.

We met Bill and Sean midday-ish. They hadn't had a rest, but were on the phone all the time. The British Embassy in Lima said Jose Henricci was arrested 29 April on a riverboat between Brazil and Peru, carrying one and half million pounds worth of pure cocaine. Two others were subsequently arrested. He could get twenty years. He was being held in Puerto Maldonado jail, two and a half hours flight from Lima. It was a hellhole in the jungle.

I went through more of Kate's paperwork. I was looking for clues, anything. Did she know what Joseph was up to? Would she have known of these plans of his? Given the sums of money at stake, I was aware how dangerous her involvement with him must have been. Could it have cost her her life?

Patrick and I slept in the afternoon. It was so unbearably hot – thank God for the air-conditioning. That evening there was no word from Bill and Sean. We went to bed at 11pm.

Sunday 22 June

We were woken by the cleaners at 8.45am. It was the first time I had overslept in how long?

Bill and Sean were already down at 9.15am having breakfasted. They had watched the Australia-England match on TV in a bar. England won! There was a Hindu ceremony in their bar, free food.

In the morning I went with Mark Wilson, the Honorary Consul, to see Maizie in her new quarters. Patrick felt quite unable to go. It was too emotional. I was introduced to Marie Claire from the embassy and her husband, Robert, who managed a nearby hotel, The Bali Dynasty. Both were very nice and – more importantly – clearly loved Maizie. On a personal level, it was wonderful to meet this eighteen-month old Weimaraner, the champion swimmer, who brought Kate so much happiness and about whom she talked constantly.

Dogs say so much about a person; it was a positive connection just being with this elegant, healthy dog whom my daughter had owned since she was a puppy. As I stroked her in greeting and she nuzzled my hand, I felt a little bit closer to Kate. Maizie was obviously very happy and very well cared for, which was an enormous weight off my mind. There was a big garden, pool and beach nearby. Any plans to move her from there suddenly seemed less likely. I would discuss this with Christian and Ruth, who had been quite adamant about the need to bring her back to the UK.

Mark Wilson's job as the Honorary Consul was a part-time position. On the way back he took me to his restaurant, the Cat and Fiddle, where I met his brother and his partner, both of whom were delightful. Sitting in a traffic jam afterwards gave me the opportunity I needed to have a frank talk with Mark who agreed with my theory about a Peruvian set-up. I told him how often Kate had said she 'hated' the Peruvians and would not let them come near her home.

He was arranging for us to meet Kate's landlord, Made Sumatra, at 11am tomorrow. We were to pack up the house and 'sort out'. Mark dropped me off at the hotel where I met Patrick for a late lunch.

At the Intercontinental, Patrick and I chose to eat in a quiet restaurant by a pool, near the beach, part of the hotel complex. It was tranquil, only a few people around. Having thought in advance that I would hate all things Balinese, I found the staff at the hotel very gentle, charming and considerate people. I was quite tearful on more than one occasion, prompting the manager – who I later discovered was called Yasa – to enquire if I was not enjoying my holiday. He did not have much English, but enough for us to convey what we were doing on Bali. He was truly shocked. Later that lunchtime he said he would like to take us to Kate's house; it was his day off the following day and he would pick us up at 10.55am.

We met Bill and Sean at 6.30pm. They had been to talk to Jenny who runs Woodstock, the bar Kate visited on the last night she was seen. They wanted to circulate pictures of Kate around the surfing community to see if they could jog any memories. Jenny suggested certain beaches where the surf would be good tomorrow and where the Peruvians might be found. Bill and Sean wanted to take pictures of both Kate and Joseph to try to get someone talking. Later they intended to do a search of the land around Kate's house, to see whether they could find any traces of her, or traces of any recent disturbance.

We discussed my fears of a Peruvian set-up. I couldn't forget that list we found on my computer at Black Dub, the names of all the people she knew to be involved in the drug trade in Bali. It was such a dangerous thing to do. Although Bill and Sean had looked into it and knew categorically that Interpol had not acted on this information, might she have told people that she had done it? I kept coming back to this; I couldn't get it out of my head.

On impulse I rang someone we had met with contacts in influential places, who might be able to help. I was told he had a great friend, who worked closely with the Australian Federal Police who were in charge of the Bali bomb outrage. He would ring that Australian contact tomorrow.

Bill and Sean were invited to have an 'English dinner' with Mark Wilson, a welcome reminder of the comforts of home for all concerned, I'm sure. Patrick and I dined quietly at the hotel.

Monday 23 June

First thing in the morning I spent a long time on the phone with Charles Orchard about posters of Kate, which I was determined to get right. I did not want to involve his wife Luli any more than she already was, as she was pregnant. We decided not to put a police telephone number on the posters, as Tri had gone to Jakarta and two others with no English were on the case! How was this going to work? I asked myself. It was just more frustration for Bill and Sean whose hands seemed to be tied at every turn.

A decision was made. They would print off copies of the poster with Mark Wilson's number at the British Consulate. Charles would arrange to have them distributed, around the bars, cafes and beaches which the surfers frequented.

Patrick and I met the hotel manager, Yasa, at 11am outside the hotel grounds and went to Kate's house. We had a meeting with Made Sumatra, the house owner, and his brother. With the little English he had, he spoke well of Kate. She was a good tenant. Always paid on time. He was convinced that Kate had paid rent after the Saturday night she was last seen. In fact he claimed to have spoken to her on 18 April. He showed us his receipt book, which quite clearly showed she paid rent on 25 April. That was a week after she vanished! My hopes soared. Of course I wanted so much to believe this, but once again I was not sure he knew what date it was today (23 June) and I was right: he seemed a bit vague on that. I didn't think he did this to be malicious: it was just a simple error. In due course this would turn out to be yet another red herring.

We went round the house and marked all Kate's stuff for shipping home. I packed up her clothes, ceramics, books and textiles and labelled up the boxes. It was a heartbreaking task. I left the kitchen stuff, bedding and towels for Ketut, who seemed grateful. Mark Wilson arrived. Ketut's husband showed Mark, Patrick and me to the internet café Kate used when she wasn't at the Hot Chillie Café. The owner was friendly enough. He said Kate used it but he hadn't seen her for ages.

We said goodbye to everyone. Ketut and I very emotional. I thought about how we had clung together when I arrived. We both thought there would be more answers by this time.

We went back to the hotel with Yasa at 2.30pm with Kate's photo albums, which we had decided to take in our hand luggage on the plane. Yasa put us down on the road outside the hotel, because as the hotel's manager it wouldn't do for him to be seen driving guests. His friendship had meant a lot to us. When Patrick and I walked up to the hotel wheeling a small suitcase, containing Kate's photo collection, we were asked by one of the front of house staff whether we had enjoyed our flight!

Bill and Sean had had a hard time. They went to Immigration who had produced a printout for 2001-2002 which was totally useless. It didn't even show journeys Kate had made. I was beginning to find this country maddeningly inefficient. Their records seem to be woefully incomplete.

Telecomecu, the mobile phone company, which Tri said he'd contacted last Friday (20 June) had now come back, saying it would take three days to get accounts – that was yesterday, Monday, so nothing had been done. XL Jakarta said we couldn't have the print out of Kate's telephone account.

Bill and Sean had paid a visit to Rodriguez in Kerobokan prison. They described him as a nice guy, caught with ecstasy, one off, not enough money to bribe the officials, so was doing time. He had lost a good job with the Brazilian Tourist Board and his girlfriend. He was very worried about Kate, but couldn't help, nobody knew anything. Or perhaps they just couldn't say anything. I had rather naively hoped for more from that meeting. I remembered Kate saying that of all the Latinos Rodriguez was one of the best. It was ironic that he was doing time in Bali's filthy jail, when so many of his associates were still living it up, enjoying the surf and much else besides.

The important contact about whom we knew nothing, rang. He could arrange a meeting with one of the Peruvian heavyweights. He would drop Bill off at this character – George's – house, but wanted to remain invisible. George was clearly prosperous: his lifestyle was light years away from the community we had encountered. He appeared to be godfather to the Peruvians. Said he spent his whole life trying to get away from South American drug dealers. He had a very nice house and was doing well. He was very sorry to hear about Kate's plight but couldn't do anything. No one on this island dared to say anything.

Bill rang our initial contact, John Aglionby of *The Guardian* whose wife worked in Jakarta for one of the mobile phone companies. They needed power of attorney to divulge these records, which we were able to supply, and would help. Bill and Sean caught up with paperwork. When we met later, Bill told me he expected to speak to the British Embassy in Peru tomorrow.

We went to bed. My chest was sore and infected.

Tuesday 24 June

Breakfast as usual with the team. We were shocked. The British Embassy in Lima said two women had been picked up with Joseph. Could Kate have been one of them? Was she alive, and if so, how terrible was her plight? I was in a state of complete turmoil, though I was aware we might have to wait a few days for confirmation.

Rang Charles to discuss posters. I felt a bit nervous about the wording on them, as we hadn't seen a proof. I was so aware we were not to make it look like a British investigation. In the end it took Patrick one hour to track them down. We agreed on printing. Luli would call in to see us with them this evening.

Bill and Sean went off with their Indonesian counterparts to the surf beaches, taking the photos with them. It was a complete waste of time. They got nowhere. People did not know them. They had not seen her before. They didn't recognize Joseph at all. It was almost farcical given that he used to surf there regularly. Once again I was struck by how frightened everyone was, scared into silence. It occurred to me later that Bill and Sean must have stood out like sore thumbs in their white shorts and sandals amidst the surfing community. You could have spotted them a mile away. No wonder the surfers closed ranks.

Came back at 1'ish. We all had lunch and waited for John Kelly, a journalist from *The Bali Sun* to come. We had decided that we needed to make as much use as possible of media, so tried to be patient when he was very late, eventually ambling along at 3.15pm. He was an unprepossessing chap, an Australian living on Bali, who seemed to me a bit of an oddball. Anyway we duly did the interview and had our pictures taken.

A woman from *The Sunday Sun* rang from Newcastle. She wanted to come to Black Dub on Friday? It seemed incredible that we would be home by then, away from here. We said yes – I felt we had to: we had to keep Kate's disappearance in the public eye.

Patrick and I rested. I felt so tired all of a sudden. All of the horror of the last few weeks was catching up with me. My throat was painful and swollen.

Luli Orchard and her friend Martha came over for early evening drinks. We had a good chat. They left at 8pm. We had baths, then supper in a poolside restaurant. The staff gave me a rose. I was very touched. The Balinese are really delightful people. They made simple, thoughtful gestures that made a difference. I understood how Kate was so taken with them.

We dreaded tomorrow, when we would get an update from Lima about those women arrested with Joseph. There was a ray of hope that Kate was alive, but in dreadful trouble.

Wednesday 25 June

We went down to breakfast feeling very apprehensive. The news was not good. Bill had spoken to Lima: the women were Peruvian; no sign of Kate. Our moment of hope that she was alive had gone. They were going to download a photo of the two women to be certain. We were all rather quiet.

Patrick and I went upstairs. I didn't feel great. I realized how much we had been hoping to hear she was with them. It said a lot about my mental state that we were 'hoping' our daughter had been caught smuggling drugs across South America.

We packed. I didn't say much. Bill and Sean had to meet local police to dot the i's and cross the t's. Official protocol must be observed at all times.

At lunchtime we sat outside for a while. I observed the beauty of the hotel's gardens – hibiscus and jasmine flowers, orchids and palms, brightly coloured birds darting around. I actually looked at it properly for the first time. I could have been anywhere for the last ten days.

I didn't want to eat. Patrick went to the poolside to sit. I went up at 2pm to have a bath and hair wash. There was a message from John Kelly of *The Bali Sun* to ring him. He read his piece over the phone.

It was really good, but there was one inaccuracy. He said Kate's passport was found at the house. It wasn't. It went missing with her. Otherwise it was a thorough and insightful piece of journalism, one of the best pieces to appear in print about Kate. I took back my initial impressions about John Kelly and made a mental note not to judge on first acquaintance.

The same 'important contact' phoned. How were we doing, was his contact helping? No. Were the Indonesian police being obstructive? Yes. I was grateful for his interest, but had to admit we hadn't got anywhere.

Again the contact rang to say he had talked to the Australian Federal Police. Bill said he had too. They would go on looking and investigating. This was important, because when the our police left Bali, we needed the search to be ongoing. It had been obvious from the outset that the Indonesian police were not conducting any sort of meaningful investigation and would probably abandon all pretence of it once we were out of their hair.

Mark Wilson from the Consulate arrived at 3pm. He was still trying to sort Kate's phone records from Jakarta, despite the fact that the Indonesian police had been saying up till now that we couldn't have a copy. Bill and Sean had to fight so hard to get those records. Now at the eleventh hour their persistence was paying off. Mark's secretary was meeting us at the airport with them.

We said goodbye and boarded the plane for Kuala Lumpur. Bill came over to me during the flight. He had been wondering whether Bruno, the lodger, had more to do with Kate's disappearance than at first thought. There were a lot of coincidences.

Bruno vanished into thin air after Kate went missing. He was found a couple of days later very drunk, having been badly beaten up. Although he had an explanation for all his cuts and bruises, it just seemed too much of a coincidence. When he was brought to our hotel in the small hours of the morning, Bill and Sean had ended up discounting him, deciding he was needy and a bit weak, but definitely not involved with her disappearance. Now Bill was beginning to question that judgment. Many thousands of miles up in the sky, he decided that Bruno Durrant needed to be brought in for questioning again, only now they would probably have to do it through international channels. I hoped we hadn't missed our chance.

We had a good flight to Kuala Lumpur where we boarded for home. It tore us apart leaving Kate there. I knew now she was dead. I didn't know how or why: I just knew it. I wished we had been able to bring her home.

We arrived at Manchester on the evening of 26 June, and were met at the airport by our son-in-law, Francis. It was wonderful to see a familiar face.

13

PERSONAL LETTERS

On 1st July we had a meeting with Bill and Sean to discuss the next steps for the investigation. We were incredibly grateful to the Cumbria Police for allowing two such senior officers to accompany us, but obviously they could not stay on the island indefinitely. Patrick and I thanked them from the bottom of our hearts. They had worked tirelessly and thoroughly, using their extensive combined skills and were an incalculable source of strength to both of us. It had been far from easy on Bali. Their hands had been tied at every turn.

They had been offered cocaine in the street, prostitutes by the policeman, who had been sent to keep an eye on them, probably to have something to use against them had they accepted, and threatened with deportation, if they so much as put a toe out of line. They had stayed on the ball, to the point, and not without humour when appropriate. Their primary job had been the investigation, but they had kept Patrick and me right, always reminding us that it was facts they were dealing with and not the rumour, gossip and hearsay, which abounded. They were far from finished and their analysts were already going through with a fine toothcomb what they had brought back with them.

Interpol were asked to investigate Bruno Durrand, who had returned to France by this stage. Although their job was to function as a liaison between the law enforcement agencies of its member countries, in practice this international co-operation was maddeningly slow. They were not good at action. In the end they did interview Bruno. They interviewed him independently and he was entirely discounted.

The phone records were a strong line of enquiry. Kate had made three calls to the same mobile phone number in the early hours of 19 April, including the last call she ever made, which was at 4.14am.

The only problem was finding out whose number it was. It seemed highly likely that the recipient of these calls was involved in her disappearance. Once again the mobile phone company dragged its feet. Apparently on Bali most people have pay-as-you-go phones and it is difficult to trace which number belongs to whom as there is no contract involved.

After several agonizing days' wait once again, we discovered that the mobile she called so many times belonged to one of two Peruvian brothers, Poca and Mario Diaz. They were friends of Joseph.

Without a body the Bali police did not accept that a crime had been committed. They were trying to regenerate tourism after the death of so many in the 2002 bombing and we were not a welcome interruption. Because of her relationship with Joseph, a known drug dealer, Kate was guilty by association. I felt strongly that the police on Bali wanted to tar her with the same brush. They did not want to know and they did not have the resources or the skills of our British police, so anything that might have been recovered by forensics in the house or her car was lost. They did little or nothing.

Bill and Sean requested that the Bali police dig up the land around Kate's house, suspecting it may have been 'a domestic' row between Joseph and Kate, which had turned violent. Although our police had searched in the adjoining area, they had not really disturbed the surface, because they had not been permitted to do so. The Indonesian police refused a more full-scale dig. They were generally obstructive.

On 2 July there was another press conference. We felt very flat. There was so little to report. When we returned from Bali, running on empty, Patrick suggested we contact a very old friend of his, a minister in the church. Dennis Donald and Patrick went back a long way. They were at school and then in the Army together at Gilgil, Kenya, before Dennis became ordained. I wasn't keen; I thought it was too soon for me, I didn't really know him and wasn't ready to talk. For the time being it was enough for me to slip quietly into a church on my own and if the church was empty so much the better. Surprisingly Patrick pursued his suggestion and made a call to his old friend.

The following day, Dennis came out to see us. I was apprehensive, but by the end of the morning I was so glad we had seen him. Once again words cannot describe how grateful to him and dependent upon his counselling we became over the next year. Thereafter, when things were getting too much, we would have lengthy conversations on the phone and at intervals he would down tools and come out to us, bringing calm and reassurance.

I was very distressed that we were unable to bring Kate's body home. Dennis made the profound observation that it is only earthly remains. He has a gift with words. Subsequently he led us through planning and preparing for Kate's service, at which he officiated.

At the time when I was leaning on Dennis so heavily, I had no idea Glenys and he had suffered the loss of a child too. Their daughter Angela had been tragically killed in a car crash some years previously. It was only when I was at a funeral some time later that I realized quite what we had been asking of him.

Very dear friends lost their youngest son in February 2004 at the age of thirty. Patrick and I went to his funeral and I was completely overcome with grief, as was Patrick. It was one of the most awful things to attend, but we felt we must do it. At that ceremony for someone else's child I realized what it must have cost Dennis to help us when he had suffered so much himself. It is rare to meet such a truly remarkable person.

One week after we returned from Bali, I was in the house and Francis was outside. A sports car drove up, a most unlikely looking woman alighted and actually nearly fell over. Extraordinary high heels and a very short tight skirt: the dogs who had not seen mutton in this form before, rushed up but sadly didn't bite her. They were probably repulsed. She demanded to speak to Mrs Osborne. My son-in-law said I wasn't at home. She persisted. He stayed his ground. She left, scattering gravel.

She rang shortly afterwards, obviously extremely miffed she hadn't seen me, to let us know her newspaper, *The News of the World*, was going to publish the most ludicrous article about Kate, all of it lies. In her piece she accused Kate of having stolen the passports of some of the victims of the Bali bomb. We were outraged – horrified at how low the gutter press were prepared to go.

Bill Whitehead had told her in an earlier phone call that it was absolute rubbish – he'd actually rung Mark Wilson on Bali to be certain that what she claimed could not have happened. Mark categorically stated that it was not possible that Kate could have done that. There was no evidence. But she went ahead with her story anyway.

We are a strong family and we'd had our resilience sorely tried in the few months before. But this woman's actions did manage to really upset us all. We'd simply had enough of Kate's life being examined, dissected, criticised when she was the victim of a crime that still remained unsolved. Christian and Ruth were particularly angry. We discussed with Bill the possibility of suing the newspaper.

It was a gloriously sunny day and I went out to deadhead the flowerbed. I found myself doing it rather energetically – imagining that one of those heads might have been hers! I always find gardening very therapeutic and I thought through everything, came into the house and Patrick and I talked. We agreed that anyone who knew Kate, and mattered, would not believe a word of the article, almost certainly wouldn't actually buy that newspaper. Those who did buy it probably knew to take the majority of its 'journalism' with a pinch of salt. We therefore decided that there was no point in suing. Anyone I had heard of, who had taken on the press, was usually destroyed; ordinary families just don't have the resources to get into litigation against the media.

Upsetting though it was, it really didn't matter. It was just words after all. Nine years later *The News of the World* would be closed down for sloppy journalistic practices, but back in 2003 they were still peddling gossip and lies if they would sell another copy of their paper. What mattered to us was finding out what had happened to Kate.

It was hard for Patrick and me to know what to do with our time on our return from Bali. I tried to go back to the beginning, to think of something we might have missed. Bill and Sean were always on the end of a phone if we needed them and always approachable, but they kept a lot to themselves. Professionally they had to. Like us, they were also the recipient of a great deal of mis-information and speculation and it was their job to sift through it all trying to find any hard evidence. However they had implied recently that they were coming round to the idea of 'a domestic'.

With this in mind I decided to go through the letters that I had found in Kate's house to try to get a better idea of her state of mind in the months leading up to her disappearance. There were a number of faxes between Joseph and Kate during one of his absences, ostensibly away at a 'surfing competition'.

Fax to Kate   14 September 2002
Hi Kate
I was waiting your call. I really don't know what to do. I want to go back, but I don't have any money. I really want to see you but I don't know, I have to stay here until I find some money to go back. I'm sorry 4 all, we keep in touch.
              Joseph
P.S. I still love you and miss you, I will try to go back as soon as possible, if not I will see what I can do. Can you call me tomorrow at 10 o'clock my time, please. I really need to speak with you. Love you.

Fax to Joseph   15 September 2002
I called both times but you were not there. I called 0630 21195. I think it's the Sorake Beach Hotel but not sure?

I'm sorry you don't have any money. It doesn't look like there is anything we can do... I guess all the forces are against us being together! It's probably for the best given everything that has happened between us. This time has been giving me some very bad memories of many other times when it has been the same. I hope you are well, and having a good time. I remember the hotel where you were staying; it's beautiful, I would have loved to stay there but couldn't afford it. I stayed down in the village in a lovely bungalow on stilts right on/in (!) the water.

You made me start thinking of you again!!!
             Take care, Kate X

For the first time, Kate did not respond to Joseph's plea for more money – little wonder given that he had been staying at a hotel she had previously considered too expensive for her means! But she did keep writing –

To Mr Joseph Attn: Mr Carlos   (no date)
Hi Joseph
I'm glad you were in touch. I'm going back to England soon. Made has sold the house and it looks like it's time for change.

My old telephone is still working but I also have a new number: 0812 367 6306.

I've tried to call you at Sorake and will try again at 4pm (your time) today. Hope that you get this and if you do that you can also read it!

If not then I will miss you – take very good care of yourself and be in contact with email when you can – it will stay 'curlykate68'
Kate X

For Kate   20 September
Hi Kate
I am very sorry to hear that u going back to England, why? Is it because u want or that u have? I don't know where u try to call me in this place cannot receive, I try both your numbers and I cannot contact, I was thinking of going back soon, but if u are going I don't see what for I gonna go there?

I don't know what to do. I still love u and think a lot about u, but the situation is not good, and I don't know when u going? …I miss you a lot. I will try to contact u soon. I still love u.
Joseph

Re-reading that letter again, I am struck by the words 'the situation is not good'. What had happened to Joseph to make him think that? He was on a remote island, more or less out of contact. He professes still to have feelings for Kate, so clearly it wasn't the situation between them that wasn't good. Could it be that he was in some sort of trouble if he returned?

A later letter from Kate tackles head on the thorny issue between them of money. She is clearly responding to a letter from him in which he accuses her of being obsessively money-minded.

Dear Joseph   (no date)

I am sure that you did not really think that I paid $5,000 to get you back here from Peru just because I wanted my money back? Why would I have wasted all my cash on all those phone calls? Why would I have been so desperate – so unhappy? Why did I always want you to swear that you were not with other women, why did I go so crazy when you never called or wrote when you said you would? Why was I so desperate when you were not coming back for Christmas? Why did I take all those photographs for you? Why did I spend so long making myself and the house look nice for when you came back? Was that because I didn't love you and only wanted my money back?

The truth seems to be the other way around. That you were only with me for money. I was your meal ticket. I could never wait to speak to you – but you could never be bothered, or forgot or whatever other excuse you used for not talking to me. I was your way out of Peru, of Centro Victoria. You knew that if you said that you loved me that that was all I wanted – so you began to tell me that again.

You have got what you wanted, a new passport paid for, a free ticket back to Bali and you had one week's free accommodation and food when you got back.

I ignored and forgave the fact that you never called me. I rationalized away all the times when you did not want to be with me, were angry with me, were violent with me – as stress – that you were under a lot of pressure. But the truth was that you hated your life, the fact that you had to be with me to get a place to stay and money – and you hated me for that. But what you forgot in all of that was that you had made me believe.

Don't blame me for taking you away from your family – you left them a long time ago. It was totally your choice to come back here. You asked me to help – and again I did. If you made the wrong decision then do not blame me for it... I know you have had an awful time. But that is not, as you said, my fault. You did not do it all for me but because you had to – to support yourself and your son, to pay back Poca, just to live...

                                        Kate

I felt very guilty reading these personal letters of Kate's, though they contained occasional phrases that might be worth investigating. With my pink marker pen I highlighted that phrase – 'to pay back Poca'. So Joseph owed money to one of the Diaz brothers as well as several others? I wondered whether that would turn out to be significant.

14

PLAGUED BY RED HERRINGS

We needed to keep going with the investigation – perhaps start simultaneously looking at some different channels. From the outset, friends of Kate had given us names of individuals and of one or two companies who could be employed to help find her. Up to that point we had been carried along on a tide of moral and practical support, steered by the evident skill and experience of Bill Whitehead and Sean Robinson. But we knew they could not stay on the case forever and then what would we do? Patrick and I began to discuss more seriously employing a private company to continue investigating the case on Bali.

Ruth had a military friend based in Kosovo, who was involved in undercover work. He was a bright chap in his thirties, whom we had met and liked. She rang him to explain the situation and the progress of the case so far. When she asked him for his recommendation, he immediately suggested Control Risks Group, a company usually employed on corporate kidnap and ransom cases which also advised on security in hot spots all over the world: Russia, South America, Indonesia, India, Pakistan, Iraq, Afghanistan and countless others.

We did our homework on them and found out what we could. They were a pretty impressive organization, highly successful in what they did. They'd been going since 1975, specializing in 'helping organizations manage political, integrity and security risks in complex and hostile environments.' I wasn't sure that crime-solving on a holiday island was their usual bag, but, aware that we had very little hard evidence to date and we were desperate so decided to arrange a meeting.

We were on the back foot. We knew we weren't Control Risks' usual sort of client; we weren't a big international case; they would probably take some convincing that we were right for them. When we met them Patrick decided to leave it to me to do the talking and, being just so impassioned I think it took them rather by surprise. I spoke forcefully and with conviction, and I knew my facts. I knew their objection would be that thousands of people go 'missing' every year and that some people in the press and on Bali thought Kate had 'chosen' to disappear. But I knew that would never happen. I told them all about Kate – her life, her passions, what drove her. I talked about the facts as we had uncovered them on Bali, about Joseph and the Diaz brothers, Bruno Durrand, the wall of silence and fear we had met. I really gave it everything and in the end talked Control Risks into taking us on.

We had a meeting with Cumbria Police on 16 July. They'd known for some time that we were considering hiring a private company to continue the work they had done on the ground in Indonesia. All agreed that it would do no harm to employ Control Risks and Bill and Sean said they would share with them their knowledge and contacts. The case as far as Bill and Sean were concerned was still wide-open and ongoing.

Following our meeting, Control Risks had done their own research into our case. As their man in Indonesia they had an Australian, a retired high-ranking police officer. He had a number of contacts connected to the drug smuggling business in Bali. He would do what he could to help. It was unfortunate that almost all his 'contacts' were associated with Joseph, leading the Peruvians to close ranks. They would not talk – some of them seemed terrified. They had their own agenda.

In my view Control Risks went after the drug angle too much, presumably because it was a world they were used to investigating. Their man talked to a lot of people involved in the underworld of Bali, and they were, one way or another, connected to drugs, but few of them really knew Kate, though they purported to do so. Though some seemed to have liked Kate, they were not about to do her any favours. They had their own backs to watch.

At the beginning of October we had a meeting with Control Risks who had completed their dossier on the case. We were all very apprehensive in the days leading up to it. Unfortunately Christian, our eldest, couldn't come to the meeting. All of us had misgivings about that – she should have been with us and now she would have to hear their findings second-hand. Ruth, Patrick and I went to the meeting, half dreading what we were about to hear.

Control Risks started off by saying how impressed they had been by the dedicated and thorough investigation undertaken by Bill and Sean, in spite of the difficulties, in a wholly unknown jurisdiction. In fact their report was not substantially different from that of our Police.

Control Risks had concluded that all circumstantial evidence pointed to Kate having been murdered by the Diaz brothers. Everyone was in agreement that they had done it. Her last phone call had been to one of them. An inflatable dinghy which went 'missing' from its beach-front location on the night of 18 April had been hired by the brothers three weeks before. Kate's body was believed to have been buried at sea.

Their report raised more questions than answers. Why would the Peruvian brothers murder Kate? Were they acting on orders from above and, if so, from whom and why? What was their motive? I knew that Joseph owed one of them money, but that would surely be a reason to go after him rather than her? Poco and Mario Diaz disappeared from Bali the night Kate was last seen. Until they could be found and made to talk, it was all speculation based on circumstantial evidence.

We went home to discuss Control Risks' findings with Christian. At long last we believed we knew who had murdered Kate, yet it seemed we were powerless to respond because we had no proof. Christian, and Ruth to a lesser degree, were very angry at the injustice. Ruth pointed out that we had photographs of the killers – taken by Kate: why not circulate them to the international press? I discussed it with John Aglionby of *The Guardian* because he had worked in the media long enough. He and Bill Whitehead were adamant that no newspaper would dare publish such a picture because of the danger of litigation.

A couple of days later, Control Risks suggested producing a press release to try to bring things to a close and protect us from journalists intruding. They sent us a fax of their proposed wording – 'Murdered by persons unknown' was the headline. We were furious, unanimous in our indignation, so they deleted that and we agreed on a formula, albeit reluctantly.

Patrick and Liz Osborne, parents of the British girl Kate Osborne who has been missing in Bali since April have stated, 'After extensive investigation into the disappearance of our daughter Kate, we are now forced to conclude that she has been murdered. We know the identities of two Peruvian suspects but cannot name them for legal reasons. It has been an unimaginably stressful six months for the whole family while we have lived in hope of Kate being found alive. We would like to take this opportunity to thank our family, Kate's and our friends, neighbours and Cumbria CID for their unfailing support which has been and is appreciated enormously. We ask that the media now respect our privacy while we try to come to terms with the fact that she is not coming home.'

It went to press the following week.

Gran constantly questioned me when I went to visit her at the home. I had to cut down the visits. I felt bad about it, but it was too painful. Somehow I managed to keep up the pretence, as Dorothy slowly deteriorated. 'When is Kate coming home?' she would ask repeatedly, even when she hardly knew who I was. She died in October 2005 not knowing of her favourite granddaughter's death.

Jen came to stay in early October. We had always been so close, shared so much, I could let my guard down with her. We stayed up late, talking about the children, about Kate, lots of good memories of us all together on family holidays over the years, the young swimming under the Branson house in their wetsuits. Happy times.

I told her about my frustrations with Control Risks' findings. That their contacts all seemed to be South Americans involved in the drug trade; the fact that everyone was too terrified to tell us anything and we were no nearer the truth. As it was, her ten-day visit saw some real ups and downs.

Jen helped me compose emails to send to Kate's friends, to ours, and to extended family, with the current situation. We had started to talk about a service for Kate – a sort of memorial. Other people had been suggesting it. I baulked at the idea of marking her disappearance with 'an occasion', but a part of me realized it might be a cathartic thing to do. I made a mental note to discuss it with Dennis Donald, our friend in the church.

Going out at all during that time was an ordeal, but a distraction. Jen and I managed it a bit with mixed results. Christian and Ruth had been very brave, both apprehensive of 'Any news?' and weary of 'How are your parents?' What about them? Kate was an integral part of us all, we all had something of her in us as we had in her.

Mid-way through Jen's visit, Kate's belongings arrived at Black Dub. Of course I had known this would happen when I arranged the packaging and shipping before we left Bali, but just having her possessions in the hallway knocked us right back. It was such a tangible sign that she wasn't coming back – so emotional, we decided to leave the actual unpacking for a few days.

On a whim I rang Jenny, who, together with her husband Eric, ran Woodstock, a popular bar on Bali. Something my sister and I had talked about stirred up a few things. We had met Jenny when we were over there and she seemed more on a level than some; at least she had been prepared to talk. Jenny said she'd started to feel threatened by the number of questions asked by journalists and by others asking questions for whatever reason. I sensed a reticence in her tone. I decided not to push it, merely asking for addresses for a couple of friends of Kate, Norbert and Gustav, both of whom I wanted to talk to further.

Gustav was a really nice guy, a clean-shaven, Dutch-American businessman. He was the one who had said that Kate knew Joseph was having an affair with a married Swedish woman and that Kate was going to confront the woman and her South American husband. Norbert was a German friend who had been paralyzed in a car accident. Kate and he had had very deep conversations together, it was a genuine meeting of minds. I called him and he was quite wonderful to talk to. Kate was so right. However our conversation was brought to an abrupt close when he said that a couple of friends of his had seen Joseph on a motorbike that morning.

I put the phone down and immediately phoned Control Risks to check that Joseph was still in jail. He was. We were plagued by red herrings.

That Saturday we went out to our first supper party since Kate went missing. I was very apprehensive, but it was with good friends and we managed it.

Out of the blue we got an email from Kate's ex-boyfriend, Stefan, with whom we had stayed on good terms. In his halting English he gave a little personal update and then asked us to note his change of email address. More importantly he wanted news of Kate. How is she? Is she happy?

It was such a shock to get his email and to hear Kate mentioned in the present tense again. He obviously hadn't received our circular telling people about her disappearance. He knew nothing. I had wondered why he – of all people – hadn't been in touch, but we had been kept so busy with the investigation, I hadn't been able to pursue it.

I felt absolutely torn up writing back to Stefan. We were very fond of him and he loved Kate – it was mutual. It was a salutary experience, choosing the right words to explain to him what had happened.

Tuesday 21 October was my birthday. Patrick, Christian and Ruth tried their utmost to make it nice for me. But it was a very hard day and I had to control the tears when I opened Ruth's card, signed from Kate too. The family was wonderful, but Kate was just so missed by us all. Missed? What does that say? I can't find words to describe how desolate we felt.

A day or so later, Ruth went down with a really nasty bug. She was totally off colour. Her glands were swollen and she took to her bed with a chronically sore throat and temperature. In her run-down state she watched an episode of *Crimewatch* on the television. Even though the crime being re-enacted had nothing to do with the crime we were dealing with, it obviously triggered her emotions. That night Ruth saw Kate in her bedroom.

Patrick and I went to see Boyd – our solicitor – a visit we had been putting off endlessly. We both found it terribly difficult – painful in the extreme – sorting out legal formalities for Kate. I don't know if it was my discomfort at having to go through this legal process or a genuine illness manifesting itself, but I felt very drained and not great at all by the time we left his office.

Patrick took charge of formalities at the bank concerning Kate's accounts. He also dealt with BUPA, the Caravan Club and various other organizations she had an interest in. We still receive mail in her name which we are now used to, and is therefore not quite as distressing as it was.

Life had become horribly surreal. One minute we were dealing with the formalities of Kate's presumed death, the next shopping for everyday items and going about the normal chores. It was very strange. I went round Carlisle feeling I'd burst into tears anytime and nearly did when Mr Gemelli, an Italian with a tailoring business locally, asked, 'How are you all?' But somewhere between shops I thought; Kate lived life to the full, experienced such happiness and gave it back to others, we had to take a leaf out of her book, follow her example and live.

We decided that it was time to open the packing cases containing Kate's possessions. Ruth and I did it together. It was lovely to see some old favourites – well-worn tops in faded silk and cotton – as well as some new things from Bali. Everything had that distinctive smell of Kate which I hoped would last forever. I was really glad to have her belongings at home. They were just 'things', but in some crucial way the essence of Kate – vibrant and alive – wafted back into Black Dub with them.

I was beginning to feel her with us at times, and then moments later felt the terrible chasm of her not being there. I hope she knows how much we love her.

We received a letter from Stefan, heartfelt and a wonderful tribute to Kate.

Dear Patrick, Liz, Christian, Ruth

It make my heart bleed to read the latest words you've sended me on the e-mail. My girlfriend, Charlotte supports me with understanding and helps me through this hard time. Kate was a wonderfull lovely person to be with. She influenced and change my life in positive ways. She helped to create the person I am today.

Kate will always be a part of me.

From the day we met I loved her and I always did and I always will.

Dear Patrick, Liz, Ruth, Christian, Francis, Poppy, Charly, I wish you from my heart lots of courage and strength to handle this sad time and the future ahead.

We all love Kate and she will always be part of us.

Lots of love,

Stefan.

We had received many letters over the past few months – lovely tributes to Kate by post and email from such diverse sources; every day brought another deluge through the letterbox. That letter from Stefan though, with its hesitant English and unusual verb tenses, really said it all. It brought back strong memories of the two of them together, Kate with that mischievous smile, teaching him English and deliberately misleading him.

Two of Kate's friends had been particularly involved in the search for Kate. Jamie Sherriff, a friend from Scotland, now married and living in London, and Francesca Fairbairn (her best friend from school days) had been completely galvanized from the start. For some time we had been talking about them coming to Black Dub. They had expressed the desire to come and see us and we encouraged them. They arrived on 1 November about nine in the morning.

I was very nervous. I'd had lots of chats with both of them over the preceding months, but found myself feeling very apprehensive as the day approached. Was it going to be all right? Would we all get bogged down with sadness? In fact I need not have worried, as we did not stop talking the whole time they were there. Looking through the photo albums was an absolute tonic. Before she left for Bali Kate had ordered and laid them out meticulously with neat labels underneath. There were pictures of Kate, Jamie and Francesca having a wild old time, as they painted the town red back in the 1980s. We had lots of laughs about some interesting haircuts and dodgy fashion decisions along the way.

We talked about Joseph a little, though I was determined not to let him creep into our day too much. Also it was impossible for me to be at all objective. Francesca made the general point that over the years with a couple of notable exceptions Kate had often made some horrendous decisions in her love life. With a shudder I thought about the man with the huskies, but there were obviously others, whom Francesca had met and who weren't deemed fit to bring home. It was hard to talk about this without Kate around to defend herself, but I had to admit there was a pattern.

As I said goodbye I felt lighter. It had been a good thing to do. They were brave to come and it worked; it was cathartic.

I'd been seeing quite a lot of Peggy Saunders. Her mother was a friend of my grandmother, which made her our oldest living family friend. Although she was ninety by then and blind, I found I could tell her about so many things. She was an artist, still sculpted and had much in common with Kate, who used to visit her regularly. There were nearly sixty years between them, but they had met as friends across the age gap.

An only child, Peggy had travelled widely and never married. When I told her what had happened to Kate I started to break down. She just said, 'Oh my dear,' placed her hand on my arm and quickly got me on to the good memories: all the textiles which they both loved. She screen-printed and did batik, as did Kate. She talked of her travels, back in the 1940s and 1950s, long before young single women were routinely jetting across the globe. She understood the need for adventure, perhaps more than anyone else. It was lovely to share those memories.

Peggy had complete empathy and she loved Kate. I could talk to her about so many things. I used to say to the family that I was 'helping Peggy out a bit' because of her deteriorating sight, but actually I think she was helping me out. Sadly she died in 2008 and we lost an old family link. You find yourself wishing you'd asked more questions, when wise people like Peggy go; there are so many things I will now never know.

Social events were still something of an ordeal. We were selective about what we went to. A small dinner party with close friends was fine, but anything larger was met with a certain amount of trepidation. I realized we were making progress when a dinner party with a friend involved the real test of lots of people, who were not such close friends, and we survived. It was a really good evening and helped with our rehabilitation.

Ruth found the social side even harder than we did. A common complaint was that people shut up about Kate when she was around. She would walk into the room and suddenly the conversation dried up. She felt that a lot of hearsay and gossip was going around, which she could not counter or deflect. They ended up talking about nothing rather than discussing the elephant in the room.

Out of the blue her cousin Elizabeth, Jen's daughter, to whom she is very close, asked her to go to Kenya with her. Her first thought was that it was impossible, she was far too busy – who would look after the horses? Almost without thinking, I said I'd do it, running the show for the three and a half weeks she would be gone. Rachel, an old friend, would be able to assist me.

That invitation to Kenya turned out to be the best thing that could have happened. Ruth was to be away for her birthday, which would be no bad thing: anniversaries seemed to be particularly hard to get through. There were only six days to go until their departure, which meant that she was forced into a whirlwind of preparations, vaccinations and packing. She did not have time to think what people were speculating about Kate.

I was kept busy looking after the horses which was just as well, for the build up to Christmas 2003 was very trying. It was hard not having Kate around at the time which she loved. From decorating the tree to wrapping presents and the fun and excitement, I felt her absence acutely. For 34 years I had chosen gifts for her in December. It seemed only yesterday we were buying her Lego sets or the Sasha doll with the long straight hair that she loved, more recently it had been those 'Red-Cross' parcels we sent to her on Bali, full of items she missed like Marmite and English mustard. A lot of the festive bonhomie grated as well. I found it best just to stick to my list of things and not linger too much in the town.

There were changes afoot on the home front too. Having lived with us at Black Dub for eighteen months, Christian and Francis had bought a house. They were moving to Low Howrigg, half an hour's drive away. They had been such a strength to us during that ghastly year, answering phones, fielding calls, vetting visitors, keeping journalists at bay, but mainly just being there. I loved having them and seeing Poppy and Charlie on a daily basis was such a tonic. I wondered what I'd do without them. As the day of the move loomed, I was determined not to get too emotional. We decided to treat it like any other day, which was a bit of a joke given the amount of work involved. Patrick did two or three trips a day for a week transporting all their gear. I did a massive clean up in the house and went a bit manic in the garden and yard, which was curiously therapeutic.

With some trepidation, a few days after that upheaval I went with Christian and Francis to the grandchildren's carol service at St Andrew's, Penrith. I wasn't sure I could trust myself not to break down in tears, when the old familiar hymns were sung. It was actually very nerve-wracking, but the service was lovely and I felt so glad I had gone. There is something very haunting, emotive, listening to children singing. Poppy and Charlie were a great source of comfort; they gave us much happiness during those dark times.

My sister, Jen, anticipated that this first Christmas without Kate was going to be fraught with difficulty, so she made a last minute plan to come and stay for five days. It was just what I needed. In between looking after Ruth's horses, which were keeping me busy, we got lots done for Christmas and even managed to invite old friends for supper one night. Looking round the table, I felt so aware how many people were helping Patrick and me on our journey.

The communication lines from Bali had gone ominously quiet. In between preparations for Christmas, I had written various letters to Mark Wilson, the Honorary Consul on the island, but hadn't heard anything. It didn't bother me at first: I was aware how much work he still had on his plate in the wake of the Bali bombings. I tried to be patient, didn't want to become a nuisance, but didn't relish lurking in the bottom of an in-tray either. For over a month he hadn't responded to any contact I had made. Surely he understood how difficult it was for us, 7,000 miles away, still no closer to knowing why our daughter had vanished. He couldn't have had that many British nationals who go missing in such circumstances.

By mid-December I was so exasperated by his silence that I rang the Foreign Office, spoke to Sarah Mannell and sent them copies of my letter to Mark. Sarah said that they had not forgotten about Kate at all. The ambassador from Jakarta was talking to the junior foreign minister as well as to the minister for foreign affairs in Indonesia. Salamudin, their director of criminal investigations had said Kate was still a priority. They had recently expanded the Department for Crime against Foreigners and she was high up on their list of unsolved cases. I felt somewhat reassured that both the Embassy and the Consulate were fully aware of our case and that no news was not necessarily bad news.

I needed progress.

On a whim I decided to ring Jenny at Woodstock on Bali. It was almost two months since we had spoken in October and I thought that she might have heard something. She was one of three people I could trust to tell me what people were saying out there, three ex-pats who had been candid with me.

Almost immediately she told me that Teresa – the western woman living on Bali with a Brazilian who was closely involved with the Peruvians – had 'lost it' in the Woodstock bar the previous Friday (Don't they all? I thought to myself). She was drunk and shouting. Said they all knew what had happened to Kate, she named the Diaz brothers. Accused her Brazilian husband and his mates of not standing up and being counted. They were all involved in it. She said that her life was in danger, that she had been threatened, but she would tell her friend at the BBC all the details, so that if she died or disappeared, the friend would know the real truth. Gesticulating wildly, she said she was terrified of the Peruvians, who had, 'Put about all the lies about Kate, a decent, innocent girl.'

After that performance in front of all and sundry, Teresa was taken home by a friend. Her husband tried to make light of it, saying that she was mad, crazy and needed help; she did not know what she was saying.

I thanked Jenny for letting me know and put the phone down, my mind racing. I was glad that the silence which had seemed to envelop the community whilst we were there, was lifting, glad also that Teresa was starting to crack up. Perhaps her guilt would get the better of her?

Having pondered Teresa's public outburst a little longer, I decided to call the Foreign Office to tell them to keep an eye on her in case she disappeared. I rang Bill to discuss it and then Control Risks, who contacted their man in Indonesia. We certainly didn't want to lose her, not now that she was starting to talk.

That wasn't the end of it. On Christmas Day the phone rang at 4pm in the afternoon. It was Teresa, sounding very agitated, calling from Bali, where it was 11 o'clock in the evening. Her husband was at Woodstock having a drink, so she was free to speak to me. She basically repeated all the statements she had made the previous week in the bar, continually going over the same accusations, naming the same names, then breaking up and becoming incoherent. She seemed to be on a mission, behaving in a very reckless fashion. She went on and on about certain people she knew for murdering a 'decent, innocent girl who did no harm to anyone.' What she was saying shocked and depressed me by turns. Teresa was on the phone for an hour and a half crying at intervals and really losing the plot. It was very distressing. In the end, when I put the phone down, I decided that I had been of more comfort to her than she had to me.

I went back to re-join the others in the sitting room and gave the family the gist of what Teresa had said. It was hard to pull crackers and enter into the spirit of Christmas again, having been harangued by a largely incoherent woman calling from the other side of the world on what was beginning to look like a crusade.

Kate had become very wary of Teresa over the course of their acquaintance. My daughter had told me of something, which happened about a year before she went missing. Kate was always prepared to like people, so when she met Teresa they became friends, of a sort. She was glad of another western woman around to talk to and occasionally socialize with. But one night Teresa rang her absolutely hysterical, begged her to 'come and get me', which Kate did, driving over despite the late hour. Teresa was in the road in her nightdress, completely deranged. Kate told her to get in the car, she'd take her back to her place, until things calmed down. Kate often took people in – letting them stay a night or two for one reason or the other. But at a junction where she was forced to slow down, Teresa leapt out of the still moving car and ran for it. After that incident Kate decided to give her a very wide berth.

Teresa was something of a loose cannon – but perhaps if she was starting to unravel, others would follow?

Throughout all this, we continued to be guided by Bill and Sean of Cumbria Police, to whom I immediately relayed this conversation. They said that the names of Teresa and her husband continued to crop up and they were looking into it. They remained in close contact with Peru, checking for any sign of the Diaz brothers passing through immigration particularly over the Christmas and New Year period. We were hopeful that the pair might make contact with their families during the holiday period, but so far there had been no sign of them travelling anywhere. In fact since the night Kate was last seen, the Diaz brothers appeared to have vanished into thin air.

15

INTERVIEW WITH JOSEPH

We felt very strongly that someone had to interview Jose Henricci, in prison in Peru, no matter what the outcome. We could not rest until this was done. Although we knew he was a compulsive liar, drug trafficker and addict there was a glimmer of hope that he might have a conscience of sorts. He and Kate had been together on and off for two years: surely he would have some feelings about her disappearance?

We were warned from all sides not to expect too much. He had been caught red-handed with four and a half kilos of cocaine, he wasn't going to make his thirteen year sentence any worse by admitting to even the slightest involvement in the disappearance of his ex-girlfriend. I thought that as a prisoner he would at least be drug-free and lucid, only to be informed that they kept the prisoners in that very remote jail on drugs, to prevent them from becoming violent. Class A drugs were routinely bought and sold within prisons of this kind.

A written request had to be sent to the judge for authorization to meet Jose Henricci, who had several aliases, and at that point was referred to as Zubiate. Permission had to be granted by the Director of the prison and there had to be prior agreement/consent from the inmate. Joseph or Zubiate agreed to the meeting, as long as it did NOT involve journalists. The Director of the San Francisco de Asis Prison, Police Lieutenant Amoretti and the Police Commander of the area, Lopez Hichicagua, were both involved in setting things up.

The prison director would facilitate adequate conditions for the meeting, which could even be conducted in his office. The relatively relaxed nature of these arrangements reflected the fact that the prison was in a remote area where procedures were less bureaucratic than they would have been in the capital.

The meeting was duly set-up. We observed all the rules and

regulations and the Control Risks man flew out from London in February, arriving in Lima with a further two-hour flight to Puerto Maldonado.

The meeting was held outside, sitting on a bench, on scrubland, surrounded by jungle. In preparation for the meeting, we had compiled, with the help of Bill and Sean, questions we needed answers to. We hoped that, if Joseph had nothing to do with the crime, and was persuaded that Kate was dead, he might be willing to help.

The immediate aim was to get as much information as possible and find something – anything – to get the case re-opened on Bali. At the moment there were no facts, but only best guesses. The starting point for the interview was – did he have any direct knowledge of Kate's disappearance? If not, assuming she had been murdered, who might have sanctioned it? We were trying to find out how the hierarchy worked among the South Americans on Bali, with particular regard to the Peruvian mafia.

As soon as Joseph appeared, he shouted waving his arms about wildly, 'You think I killed Kate, I not kill Kate. I love Kate.' Those sentiments were expressed several times throughout the interview. He had to be placated and, when calmer, spoke in reasonable pidgin English. When excited, he reverted to Spanish.

Joseph was cautioned that he would be questioned but was not obliged to answer the question, if he did not wish to do so. It was explained to him that we, Kate's parents, needed to know what had happened to our daughter. He said he understood what was being said, but couldn't help because he 'knew nothing'.

He referred to Kate in the past tense, but tried to persuade the interviewer that she was alive and somewhere in South America. Later he said she would be on some island in Indonesia laughing her head off.

He admitted he owed Kate some money and claimed he was a hugely successful drug dealer. When he was asked why he had not therefore paid Kate back, he made no reply.

He made statements and then contradicted himself. He said Kate had moved heaven and earth to get him out of rehab in Peru. (In fact we knew that he had made all the running and pleaded with Kate to get him out of 'the hell-hole'.) Throughout he ranted about his love for Kate, but implied he knew she was dead. He tried to implicate her in everything he had done.

At the suggestion that Mario or Poca Diaz might have killed Kate, Joseph laughed outright. So who might have been responsible for the murder he was asked? Silence.

The only revealing thing he said was that Kate had downloaded numbers from his phone and rung around, telling the people concerned that she was going to expose them for drug dealing – if it was true.

When asked who the main man was behind any plan to kill Kate, Joseph said, 'I don't know his name. He is an Indonesian man, his nickname is "Wawan". He lives on Bali.' When asked who gave the order to buy drugs for the syndicate, he answered, 'Marco'. He was the man who spoke with Wawan.

It was explained to Joseph that Kate's last telephone call was to Poca. This was obviously critical to the investigation. Did Poca kill Kate? 'No – it was not Poca.'

So who was it?

'I tell you these things and I will end up dead. These people are very bad people.'

In the event, this so-called interview was an absolute farce. Joseph claimed to be successful at what he did. He also described himself as a professional surfer, who competed in various surf competitions. If that was true, why didn't he repay Kate instead of freeloading and 'borrowing' extremely large sums of money from her? The total he owed her when she went missing was in excess of £20,000. It seemed he was not only a compulsive liar, he was also deluded.

He nearly fell off his chair laughing at the possibility of the brothers murdering Kate. Apparently there was no way those two would do such a thing. Why would they? They had nothing to do with drug smuggling: photography was their business, editing videos of surfers.

The only inkling he gave that he might know more than he was letting on was when the conversation turned to that list of numbers

Kate may have taken from his phone. What he said about that – and that alone – had a ring of truth about it. If she had done as he said, she would certainly have been in great danger.

Apart from that it was completely and utterly unproductive and totally implausible, except possibly for one thing. When he saw the photos of Kate that we had sent, reportedly he shed some tears and said he had loved her.

The picture they took of him in the jail shows him with his hands flung out to the side, his eyes staring fixedly, pupils dilated. He appears wired and manic. I can hardly bear to look at it.

The man from Control Risks came to Black Dub and told us all this, while I made notes.

We had also wanted to ask Joseph whether he thought he had been set-up. Where exactly was he discovered with the cocaine? Could he have been deliberately shopped? Perhaps the plan was to dispose of both Joseph and Kate simultaneously? Who might have informed on him? It was certainly a coincidence that he was arrested about three weeks after she vanished forever. These questions and more we had wanted to ask Joseph but they were not raised.

This was the end of the road it appeared; we were bereft.

After six months of employing Control Risks, we all decided we could do no more. Their man in Indonesia, who had been handling the case, said he would continue to investigate in his own time.

But for Bill and Sean the case was still open and they were continuing with enquiries through Interpol and in any other way they could think of. They largely discredited Joseph's claim that Kate had downloaded the telephone numbers; in their opinion he had almost certainly made that up.

There have been various theories as to what happened to Kate that night of 18/19 April 2003. It is known that she got dressed up for a Saturday night out with friends. She told her maid that she 'was going to get her money back'. She had drinks at the Woodstock Bar. Sometime after midnight she dropped a Dutch friend called Ernst off at his house and they sat in her car and talked. He would have liked to invite her in, but he was too scared of the Latinos to be seen stepping on their 'territory'. After this we do not know what Kate's movements were, only that she made several calls to the mobile phone of one or other of the Diaz brothers, the last one being at around 4 o'clock in the morning.

Everyone agreed that in all probability Kate had been murdered by the Peruvians, for whatever reason, but probably because of orders from an Indo-Chinese or Latin American high up in the drug trade. There was enough circumstantial evidence to suggest that she had been buried at sea.

A dinghy had been hired by the two Diaz brothers three weeks before Kate was killed and it was stolen the night of her disappearance. Her car, with a flat tyre, had been dumped at the airport, obviously to mislead, and so many lies and misinformation had been put about to cover tracks that – combined with the incompetence and obstruction of the Indonesian police – it was impossible to positively accuse anyone.

Bill and Sean had met a number of people on Bali who offered a variety of theories as to what may have happened to Kate. It was difficult to evaluate the information without corroboration, and even more difficult to evaluate the credibility of those giving the information. Some seemed simply to want to play a part in the drama, a few wanted money and many were clearly just wasting our time. Some of these people seemed sincere, whilst others exhibited distinctly eccentric behaviour, which detracted from their theories. The majority seemed extremely frightened.

In 2006 someone came forward to tell us that Kate had met her death following a confrontation with 'a Swedish woman', mother of several children. Kate had been heard to say she was going to 'have it out' with a Swedish woman about her relationship with Joseph – the woman having had an ongoing affair with him.

The person coming forward said the woman had set Kate up. Her motive was jealousy. She was jealous of the time Joseph and Kate had spent together and the fact that Kate was seen by many as his partner. She need hardly have worried, since Joseph was by then an ex-boyfriend of Kate's.

It is also possible that Kate was jealous of the married woman who was having an affair with her part-time boyfriend. From the letters I have read, it seems that Kate had not stopped loving Joseph, although it is hard to contemplate after everything he had done to her, stolen from her and put her through. Kate could be possessive, fiery, very hot-headed and perhaps she did accuse the woman and threaten to tell her husband. It is feasible. She may have been going to tell the husband, a man further up the Latino mafia than Joseph. No man likes to hear that his wife is being unfaithful. That would have put both Joseph and his Swedish mistress in a very dangerous position.

This last theory, focusing around the Swedish woman, had a degree of corroboration, but again unfortunately there was no hard evidence. Bill and Sean were of the opinion that this fitted with other information they had and was the most likely solution. We were also told that Kate's body had been put in a surf bag, wrapped in heavy chains and buried off a deep shelf at sea. We did not have a hope of finding it.

We were fairly sure we knew what had happened, but it seemed we could not do anything about it. Christian and Ruth could not believe that the Swedish woman could not be brought in for questioning. The police did arrange for someone to watch the movements of the woman and her husband, when they were leaving Bali and on their return to Sweden, but they were never caught with anything.

Bill and Sean tried to enlist the assistance of the Australian Federal Police by employing covert techniques which are commonplace in the UK, subject to the appropriate authority being obtained. The Australian Police said they were still dealing with the aftermath of the Bali bombing and at such a time did not regard this case involving a British national as a priority for them. What wonderful international co-operation, I thought to myself!

Over the years we've had letters, phone calls in the middle of the night, emails, tip-offs, informants: you name it, we've had it. We've had to get used to the fact that people will come out with the most outlandish theories, suppositions, opinions and mindless gossip. We just had to take whatever was coming. If anything, I've become less judgmental. Sometimes the most unlikely-sounding people have come up with the sanest opinions. It seems to be my job just to hear it, to take the information on board, to sift through and to try to sort the sense from the nonsense.

We've had to be prepared for anything. People have come out of the woodwork peddling all sorts of hearsay. 'Kate's still alive' was a call I had only a couple of years ago. You realize you've got a complete fantasist on the phone. People email us saying they can help, but actually it's money they want. It still shocks me that that there are people out there looking to profit from our misery. I've listened to so much terrible stuff, because one day someone might come through with something sensible or concrete, a scrap of evidence that could lead to an arrest.

16

SERVICE OF CELEBRATION AND THANKSGIVING

We had been meeting regularly with Dennis Donald. He had been immeasurably helpful on so many levels. As a Christian minister, he has supported me in my faith, but he has also shown great compassion as a father, who tragically has been there before us. I don't know where Patrick and I would have been without him.

With his guidance we planned the Thanksgiving Service for Kate on 17 April 2004, exactly a year to the day that she went missing. I had blown hot and cold on whether I could handle such a final tribute, but in the end was persuaded that it would be a positive step. Countless friends of Kate had written to us during the past twelve months, shocked by the news, asking to be updated on any developments, wanting to help in any way they could. This service would be as much for them as for us. I tried to write back to anyone who emailed or contacted us, inviting them to 'A Service of Celebration and Thanksgiving for Kate'. There were too many people to call, so I did my best and hoped that word would get around. There were many of Kate's friends we were never able to contact, as they had changed their email address and Kate's address book had gone missing with her.

On Dennis' recommendation we decided that the service should be in St Cuthbert's, Carlisle, and afterwards at The Tithe Barn. Part of me had wanted it to be in our local church in Brampton, but it just wasn't as accessible. We were unsure whether there would be one hundred or three hundred people attending so were reassured to know that St Cuthbert's had the capacity if we needed it.

Since Christmas we had done our utmost to focus on the service. Dennis had been wonderful, helping us with the format and gently keeping us right. We had very strong views as to what we wanted, based on Kate's own loves, so it was not difficult in the physical sense for joy to be the overriding theme. She was so full of life and laughter and that was what we wanted the service to reflect. Poetry and music were obviously vital. Spiritually it took a heavy toll, but having to concentrate on the uplifting aspects of Kate's life, which were many, enabled us all to shrug off a little of the gloom of the preceding year.

Once again the family was amazingly strong. I am indescribably proud of Patrick, Christian and Ruth, and then there was Jen (my sister), Tana (Patrick's sister), old school friends Jamie Sherriff and Francesca Fairbairn and a lovely boy called Edward Greenwood, who had met Kate during a stay on Bali and kept in touch, returning to stay with her. When he made contact with us, we asked him to say something. It took enormous courage for everyone to participate in the service as they did, especially Edward, who did not know anyone else there. He spoke for other friends in Australia, who were unable to be there. They wrote to us at Black Dub saying Kate had looked after them in dire times and they were devastated at her death.

We heard from an American artist, Charli, who had been a true friend of Kate's on Bali but sadly had left the island two weeks before that fateful night in April. Control Risks had managed to track her down in Paris and she sent us a letter which said, 'Kate was a wonderful and dear friend to me. I was having a very bad time and she gave me true friendship. I gave her a painting for sheltering me and guiding me through a dark period of my life.'

So many letters expressed a similar gratitude for what Kate had done for them at a bad time. I felt very proud of her ability to show compassion so widely and to make others feel good about themselves, but I wished there had been a little more love and self-protection left over for herself.

I hoped that readings at the service would go some way to explain what it was in Kate that drove her. She inherited genes from a long line of adventurers; innately compassionate people, with a missionary instinct and deep convictions. Kate's ancestors were a mixed bunch. Often not easy people, they felt compelled to follow their chosen path, even if it was at odds with the society they lived in.

Patrick spoke for both of us, words we had prepared together. The past year had been as harrowing for him as it had for me, though we had tackled it differently. He too felt the service was the right thing to do – he described it as 'a milestone in the journey which would never go away.'

When we were drafting the address we endeavoured to be honest and forthright, and, in doing so, felt it was the best tribute we could make to Kate. We wanted to paint a picture of the vibrant, artistic, complex girl she was. Our daughter stands as an example to us, having taught both Patrick and me much about life, to laugh at ourselves, the irrelevance of some western values and the virtue of loving deeply and honestly, of friendship and loyalty.

Heartbreaking though it was, it seemed the right thing for Patrick to make the speech about the daughter he had loved so much. He had a natural way with words and a clear speaking voice, which faltered only slightly at the beginning. We had given Dennis Donald a copy of the speech as well in case it became too much for Patrick, but it didn't.

Patrick's Address

Kate was a pioneering spirit. Her distinguished ancestors included a seventeenth century naval hero who fought in the Napoleonic Wars, later freed 420 slaves in a battle off the coast of Africa and was afterwards instrumental in establishing settlements in New Zealand.

Two others, Kate's great great aunts, were some of the first women doctors in Britain. One of these, a missionary, translated the Bible into a Berber (Arabic) dialect whilst living with the Tuareg in Central Sahara; this same missionary also happened to be the English diving champion in 1905.

Kate's great-grandparents worked on the Labrador setting up medical missions for the Eskimos and Indians in the early twentieth century. Her great-grandfather, a passionate climber, was on the 1922 Everest Expedition.

Liz's mother was a glider pilot and WAF Officer during the Second World War, and rode powerful motorbikes.

These then were her antecedents, Kate herself had a passion for travel, from Canada, North Africa, India, South America and Indonesia where she finally settled on the island of Bali. She was intensely interested in people from every sphere and culture. Through her love of photography and graphic letters, Kate introduced us to places we could not otherwise have imagined.

Never one to back down she'd be the first to blow the whistle at any perceived injustice involving people or animals. Always ready to stand up and be counted, combined with the sometimes-childlike quality in her nature was a dangerous combination. The life she lived was not without risk.

On a personal level, Kate was loving, loyal, difficult, hugely talented, vital, maddening, brave and compassionate. She had a wicked sense of humour and was the most enormous fun. Extremely gifted artistically, she could turn her hand to anything from making wooden furniture, interior design, installing her own bathroom to illustration, photography and car maintenance.

Kate was the ultimate free spirit. She remained true to herself throughout her life which took courage. We have much to learn from her. She has left a huge legacy of love and inspiration.

She knew that she was loved by us as she unreservedly loved her family. It is a privilege to be her parents.

When Patrick finished there was complete silence. Then Dennis, who was officiating at the service, said, 'I hope you'll never have to do anything harder than that.'

Jamie Sherriff then got up to the lectern. He was an old school friend of Kate's and had helped immeasurably during the investigation, providing names, addresses and an introduction to the Orchard family, who helped us so much during our stay on Bali.

'Curly Kate'
Just seeing the photographs of Kate on the back of the service sheet makes me smile. She was a wonderful smiler and whenever I conjure up Kate in my mind now, she has a big fat smile on her face or a cheeky grin.

Her humour, her presence was indicative of who she was – wry, giggly, a truly infectious being, a joy to be around. There are many tales to share about Kate's life and all of you who knew her can remember how amusing and naughty she was. Known to cram a week or so's work into one night she always produced the most amazing graphic results for her bosses. Cheeky, yes, but so sure of her talent she was able to reap the best harvest.

Kate never failed to enthrall us with her enthusiasm for life. She touched all of us and on occasions certainly frightened Patrick and Liz; such as when the XR2 was wrapped around yet another tree or dipped into a ditch. Losing count was the best way to deal with these glitches as insurance costs soared. It was much to their relief that in came the camper can and more concentration was given to negotiating first gear to second and not one hand with fag in it, another holding a steaming mug of coffee. Those of you local to here would have been much relieved that her taxi driving days were short lived. Her cars were an extension of her life. Press a button and the entire living room would pop out, comfort and cosiness were the order of the day.

All sweet and shy: not a bit of it. Nothing was hidden for long though, and much to the envy of her school friends she was always the first to participate or break free. Here was this Amazonian creature who captured the hearts of many but never let it taint her shell as she felt it wasn't warranted. While completely oblivious to any approaches, on the other side of the coin she knew exactly what she wanted. Easy to please but never one to suffer fools gladly. Hence her determination to pursue the truth and what was rightfully hers, led her to her disappearance.

Kate was far from conventional and she took enormous risks to be herself, wilfully independent, a mender of broken souls.

Why did she choose this path?

Always on the move, travelling around the globe, forever the adventurer like her ancestors. Being able to enjoy the freedom of her life and certainly living an existence that took her to pastures far and wide to feed her soul, she was able to quench her thirst and give many what they did not have the courage or willingness to do.

Kate was free in our eyes. Whenever I saw her again there were no awkward moments but a smile and the sense that time had stopped while she was away and what a pleasure it was to see her again.

I am grateful for knowing Kate – an untapped force never to be thwarted, so refreshing to be around and so willing to set you straight over a nice cup of tea or chat about nothing.

The chance to talk to Patrick, Liz, Christian and Ruth over the last year about Kate has made me realize how Kate's spirit lives on. The discussions we have are very restorative, creating enormous feelings of happiness and moments of sadness. She was special, albeit unaware of this, and the impact of her loss illustrates how much she enhanced our lives.

Her absence is very real to all of us and Kate's family will carry on searching until there is certain completeness in their hearts. My feelings are with them for the times to come.

Thus wherever you are Kate, you are always in our thoughts – happy ones.

Christian, Ruth, Jen and Tana all gave readings beautifully.

Dennis Donald, who was introduced as a friend of the family, made the point, poignantly, that he also shared with Patrick and me the experience of losing a grown-up daughter – 'We should go ahead of our children' he said.

And here we are, trying to cope with a strange turmoil of celebration and sadness. Kate would surely want us to be ourselves. If there is laughter at the memories, that is just as right as the tears which come from the pain of having loved and lost her.

It's a year since Kate's disappearance on Bali. Twelve long months of searching. For her family a year of agony, of longing, of hoping and then settling into the numbing acceptance that Kate has died.

Which brings us to today – a gathering of family and friends, literally from around the world – a gathering which has come about from no single decision, but rather from a collective urge to get together and surround Kate's memory in an act of love and celebration.

(Extract from Dennis Donald's address)

Edward Greenwood, one of Kate's many friends from her travelling days, gave us a heartfelt recent memory from her time on Bali.

I didn't know Kate for very long. You all knew her for so much longer than I did.

I speak for two other people who can't be here today who she took in, looked after and showed the wonderful island of Bali. In my mind I will always remember Kate as a warm, colourful glow on the beach at Dreamlands. I remember her beautiful house at Uluwatu and how much she loved her dog. I'm tremendously proud to say that she was my friend and I miss her.

I hadn't met Edward before, but there was something about him with his youth (he was much younger than Kate) and sensitivity, which reminded me of the journalist, Rageh Omaar. His address was short, but poignant, a vivid reminder of the life she had chosen for herself on Bali.

Seven hundred people came to the service at St Cuthbert's Church, Carlisle, family and friends, all united by the fact that they really loved Kate. I tried to talk to everyone, but it just wasn't possible. It meant a lot to me the journeys people had made to get there, some coming from distant corners of the globe, others closer, but still having made a tremendous effort to be there.

Detective Chief Inspector Bill Whitehead and Detective Inspector Sean Robinson were of course there, as was the man from Control Risks. Afterwards, back at The Tithe Barn, Bill and Sean played with Poppy and Charlie, my two grandchildren, now aged eleven and nine and all too aware of what had happened to their beloved aunt.

Sadly Stefan, Kate's old boyfriend, was absent. He was in New Zealand at the time and could not afford the airfare. He made up for it with his own personal ceremony which also took place on 17 April. Some time later he sent us a picture of himself in a boat putting out to sea, holding a bunch of brightly-coloured flowers ready to cast them on the water. Right at the moment the picture was taken, the rain eased up, the sun came out and a rainbow can clearly be seen in the background.

ON THE WRITING OF THIS MEMOIR
July 2014

Since Kate died, I have known that sooner or later I had to put her life down on paper. In October 2009, with winter approaching and no gardening to distract me, the time was right. I set up a writing space on the dining room table with everything I needed to make a start. I re-read all the letters which had been sent to us, had beside me the cards Kate had made over time and embarked on 35 years of memories. It was only when I came to her first adventure abroad that I remembered I had kept all her letters from her travels. I looked them out, read them all over again and that was my inspiration to try to publish this book. What had begun as a need to record Kate's life, an attempt to write a personal tribute to her, had become a mission.

Over the previous months I had deliberated where to begin, how best to tell the story of Kate. Once I had made the decision, the writing flowed. However, I am not a professional author and, given the intensely emotive subject, I was not hugely confident of my ability to do it justice. During times of self-doubt – and there have been many – Patrick has been an absolute rock, although initially he wasn't sure I could do it. I would read extracts to him, asking for reassurance, or give him a few pages to read. For him, it was not the cathartic experience I had hoped for, nor was it for Christian and Ruth. Patrick was reluctant to think about things he had put away. But I needed him and he was there for me. I hope that, when I have put it all together, they will pick it up from time to time and smile and laugh at the good times, of which there were many.

I told few people at first, apart from the immediate family, what I was proposing in case I failed. I also told Bill and Sean of Cumbria Police, whose response was that they always knew I would write a book about what had happened. As time went on I told a few friends that I had begun to write about Kate. I had read somewhere that if you are thinking of writing a book, tell a few people, because the fear of failure motivates you to actually do it.

My motive was that I thought it would be cathartic and actually I have found it an uplifting experience, with the exception of the last few chapters. There has been a calming effect in organizing the last fifteen years into some sort of order, even if there has been little of what our contemporary society likes to term 'closure', a word I dislike intensely. How does anybody 'close' or put an end to something like this?

As it evolved, quite naturally it became a tribute to Kate, which is what I was seeking. But I would also like it to be a tribute to the rest of the family, particularly Christian and Ruth who have been indescribably strong, involving us in their lives and keeping us going. Francis together with Poppy and Charlie, very caring children, have played no small part.

Since the memorial service, Ruth has moved into a house beside us, here at Black Dub, where she lives with her twins, born in 2011. So now her hands are full with two lovely children – Arthur and Honor – rather than horses and competitions. I, too, get to help out, when things become too much. It's wonderful her being just over the yard from us. But when she gets low even now, it's definitely Kate she misses and it is the same for Christian. When Ruth's boyfriend was killed in a fishing accident a year after Kate's death, Ruth said 'I thought Kate would look after me.'

I'm sure it is true to say that people do not realize how much siblings suffer and are affected by the death of a sister or brother – it is painful, deep, and insidious. Very often their grief is suppressed by the parents' needs and with siblings it can take a long time to come to terms with such a tragedy. I've tried to remember this in relation to my daughters.

We see Stefan fairly regularly – he's always welcome here. He came to stay a year or so after Kate disappeared. He walked through the door and gave me one of his great hugs. It was very emotional for all of us. He's still full of little gestures, which mean a lot. He found a four-leaf clover and tucked it into a framed photograph of Kate which Tobi Corney took. He is not such a wanderer these days; in fact he's ready to settle down now: just got to find the right girl.

Bali remains a place I feel very ambivalent about. It's often in the news. They caught the Bali bombers over time; all were members of a violent Islamist group backed by Bin Laden. Just recently the island made the headlines again with a middle-aged British woman caught bringing drugs through immigration. She led the police to her 'syndicate' in return for leniency. Now there are four of them awaiting trial with the possibility of the death penalty. On one hand I'm astonished that people can be so stupid, so greedy; on the other I can't help wondering when I'll see some of the Latino names we heard bandied around in jail for trafficking.

Since 2003 we have been dragged into a world of tabloid journalists, informers, drug smugglers; we have been so far out of our comfort zone on many occasions. We've kept lines of communication open because we still hold out hope that one day we'll find out what happened and why, and that the people involved will be brought to justice.

These days I cannot stomach anything remotely violent on the television or in the cinema. Patrick and I went to see the film *Master and Commander* about eighteen months after Kate died. I found it unbearable – all those bloody Napoleonic battles, bodies over the side of ships – it was too close to home. I can just about take detective dramas, sometimes.

Bill and Sean are in touch with us from time to time. They have separately gone on to work on numerous high profile cases for the police, but nothing bugs them as much as Kate's disappearance, which remains unsolved more than a decade after it happened. The man from Control Risks contacted us by email last year. He said he'd remained 'fascinated' by the case and would be keen to investigate further on Bali if we were interested.

While writing this book, certain things became clearer to me; Kate's wonder at so much in life, things of beauty – be it landscape, art, music, dance, children – she was childlike. She was so switched on and yet could be so taken in.

I can see her now in her thirties, leaning against the Rayburn in the kitchen, mug of tea in hand, a cigarette in the other. That lovely smile, guileless and open, inviting people in.

I recognize so much of myself in her, the gullibility; I was, and am now, occasionally the cause of great mirth, as when Patrick and I were driving north on the M6 and he pointed out the Bullring. I responded with horror, 'They don't have bullfighting in Birmingham, do they?'

The volatility for sure came from me. My grandmother warned me at the age of twelve that no one would ever marry me, if I didn't learn to curb my temper. Fortunately boarding school helped. Kate's wit to a large extent came from Patrick and the two shared an earthy sense of humour and were great lateral thinkers.

I was quite miffed when our vicar, who had a long friendship with my family, told my future mother-in-law on our engagement that perhaps married life would settle me, because I was wild while growing up. It was true.

We were encouraged, just as I urged the girls, never to be afraid of being individual, of breaking the mould, as long as it didn't hurt anyone. It can take courage not to conform, to dare to be different, to do your own thing and I remember clearly the longing to be free until I was about 30, in spite of the fact, or perhaps because, I was married at nineteen and had two children by the time I was 24. A romantic ideal about the gipsy life stayed with me for a long time, but I never was as brave, nor as true to myself as Kate. I did not have the same mental and physical resolve.

I could empathize with Kate's interest in spirituality. I have also always been interested in exploring different forms of religion. I treasure those night-time sessions we had, down in the sitting room in the early hours, chatting about the search for life's meaning.

We were very similar in many ways. I always have been easily moved by music, dance and art, albeit that my taste is more conventional than Kate's. Actually, her image often belied the fact that she was very traditional in her views on many things. After her death it was especially hard going to children's plays, concerts and carol services or even watching them messing about; it was so evocative and I struggled to contain myself. Writing about Kate's childhood, replaying it, re-living all those dramas, has helped. No one can take that away.

There have been so many tears, so much anguish; some days it all seems very raw and unresolved. Many times I've had to tell myself to get a grip, to put on a brave face. I felt there was a limit to how much people wanted to hear and, in order to make it easier for others, I sometimes pretended things were okay when they weren't. One of the worst moments for me has been when a stranger asks that innocuous question, 'How many children do you have'. It's impossible to say 'two' and deny Kate's existence, so I say, 'Three, but one died.' Usually that's the end of the conversation, but once someone pursued it. Fifteen years on, there are no words to describe the pain, the longing, the loss. A friend whose sister died told me that their mother said it was like an unquenchable thirst. She's right.

I have loved writing about Kate and could go on forever; people have said everyone has a story about my daughter and it's true. Many of them have found their way into this memoir via anecdotes and letters. Lots of them made me laugh out loud, recounting one or other escapade. Some were unprintable. All bore her trademark need to make the next adventure even better than the last.

Kate herself has helped me write this; her passion for life, her wicked sense of humour and her deep love remain inspirational. It's a wonderful legacy.

We are so grateful to have had Kate for thirty-five years.

Elizabeth Osborne,
July 2018